The Saint Joseph's Day Table Cookbook

Recipes and Traditions of the Giordano Family

Chef Mary Ann Giordano

With Paul B. Giordano, M.D.

Photography by Nica Jadoch

BUFFALO
HERITAGE
UNLIMITED

Buffalo, New York

BUFFALO
HERITAGE
UNLIMITED

For information about reproducing selections from this book, contact
Permissions, Buffalo Heritage Unlimited, 266 Elmwood Avenue #407, Buffalo, NY 14222

www.BuffaloHeritage.com

Text by Mary Ann Giordano

Photography by Nica Jadoch

Book design by Dr. Mark Donnelly

ISBN 978-0-9825745-9-1

Printed in the United States of America

10 9 8 7 6 5 4 3 2 1

This book is dedicated to. . .

My grandmother, Josephine Giordano, who, with her sister, "Aunt Ange," carried on the tradition of the Saint Joseph's table observed by their parents in the town of Montedoro, Sicily, where it was called la tavola di San Giuseppe.

My father, Paul B. Giordano, M.D., who keeps the Saint Joseph's table tradition going and who has encouraged me to learn about its symbols, stories, and recipes. He suggested that I write this book and led me through the process. Cooking with my father, planning the parties, and writing this book with him has been a truly memorable experience.
His love of food has shaped my life.

And to the generations that came before me and the generations that will come after me.

Contents

Introduction

Saint Joseph's day, March 19, is a favorite holiday of my family, not because we are devout Catholics, but because we are a family of chefs. And Saint Joseph's day is a day of feasting from a buffet of traditional foods served in traditional ways with special observances in honor of the earthly father and guardian of Jesus. We revere our ancestors and honor their traditions, recipes, and cooking practices.

As we researched to enhance our own Saint Joseph's table, we found that there was not a single book available to help us prepare for this important event. So we decided to write a cookbook that would help anyone who wishes—be it an individual, a family, or a small group—host their own Saint Joseph's day celebration in a manageable way by providing appropriate recipes, prayers, and symbols for making a Saint Joseph's table.

By means of this age-old tradition, you, like generations before you, can honor your ancestors, remember your friends and relatives, pray for good luck. . . or thank San Giuseppe for the good fortune you have already enjoyed.

Traditionally, Saint Joseph's day feasts are designed to feed a multitude—indeed, the whole community in the town square. Custom called for the better-off residents of the community to share the burden of making the table and supplying the food. Everyone took part in the celebration and tasted from the table. Here in the United States, it is common for churches to host large-scale celebrations where their parishioners contribute the food for, and decorate, a large, elaborate buffet. Usually, guests are invited to partake of the table for a small donation, but no one is turned away. Some restaurants also host a Saint Joseph's table, charging a plate fee for the event. But if an individual or family unable to pay were to show up to share in the feast, it would be in very poor taste to refuse to serve them.

The recipes included herein are meant to serve a party of twenty to thirty people in a home or other small venue. Adjustments can be made for a larger or smaller celebration by adding or removing dishes. But please be sure to include your own family favorites, and you may wish to double the recipes for these.

Our altar is not as large or elaborate as those sometimes used by others; most of the symbols are represented in a tasteful but somewhat understated manner. Again, we are attempting to guide you in hosting a celebration that you can comfortably do on your own.

My Family

The Giordanos are a family of cooks, chefs, and farmers—some are professionals, some are amateurs who perform only at home for their own enjoyment. It's no surprise, really, for my family's stories were centered on food, and life was lived in the kitchen. I recall that even as a toddler the smells of freshly baked bread, a pot of sauce on the stove, and heaps of greens of some sort being washed in the sink filled the kitchen and attracted me. I remember, too, that when I was ten, my fourteen-year-old cousin Bernard, who lived across the street, came to stay with us for the weekend, just so my father could teach him how to make chocolate mousse.

When I was a child, my 85-year-old grandmother, Josephine, once stopped bulldozers from clearing a field for the construction of a house while she and her 82-year-old "baby" sister picked the cardoons (burdocks) that were growing wild in the field. Everyone older than forty in my family carries a knife and a paper bag under their car seat, just in case they spot a patch of dandelions or *erba mari* on the side of the road. In my family you work hard, save your money, never throw anything away, and take nothing for granted. We came from poor families in Sicily, and even though my father and uncles all did very well financially, they still cook like they're thankful for every crust of bread. Such is the wonder of our ancestral recipes!

In addition to my almost thirty years as a chef in the restaurant industry, I have a bountiful culinary background rooted in my family and ancestry. My grandmother, Josephine Alaimo, was born in Montedoro, Sicily, in 1894, where she lived until she immigrated to America at age eleven. Crossing the Atlantic Ocean aboard the steamer "Neapolitan Prince," she arrived at Ellis Island in New York City on July 23, 1905, together with her mother, Paolina, two sisters: Maria and Angela, and two brothers: Gregorio and Salvatore. Grandmother married another Sicilian immigrant, Carmelo Giordano, who was born in 1893 and immigrated from Bivona, Sicily, to the United States through Boston. Together they raised six children, four of whom entered the culinary field.

Food made my family tick then and it still does. My father's love of cooking directed my brother's and my careers toward cooking—we are both chefs. My family shares that love of cooking . . . as well as the love of tradition. So it is only fitting that I write the cookbook that my father has always said needs to be written.

Over the past fifteen years, my family and I have hosted many Saint Joseph's day celebrations. We have researched numerous sources both here and abroad, collecting traditions, recipes, and symbolic meanings from countless sources. We have tested recipes on large groups and documented our research both in writing and photographs. I am proud of our work and our heritage.

As a third-generation Italian American, I fear that my generation is losing touch with the recipes and traditions important to and enjoyed by our ancestors.

This book is my effort to reclaim some of those recipes and traditions and to ensure that they remain available for my children and their children.

In 2005 my father and I made a *Tavola di San Giuseppe* (Saint Joseph's table). During the blessing of the table, I prayed to *San Giuseppe* to bless my family with a child. We did not have a table in 2006, but in 2007 the honored guest at our Saint Joseph's table was my 15-month-old adopted daughter, Gabriella Mirsa. My prayers had been answered more quickly than I could have known, for Gabriella was conceived in March 2005, the same month in which we held our table. So it is with this granted favor in mind that I write this cookbook to preserve the Saint Joseph's table and pass on its symbols, traditions, menus, and recipes.

History of St. Joseph's Table

Saint Joseph (*San Giuseppe*), the earthly father of Jesus, is the patron saint of Sicily. His feast day is celebrated on March 19.

The Saint Joseph's table is a tradition dating back to the Middle Ages when there was a severe drought in Sicily. No rain fell, no crops grew, and countless people died in the resulting famine. The peasants prayed to God for rain, but they also prayed to Saint Joseph to intercede with God on their behalf. They promised Saint Joseph that if God caused it to rain; they would hold a special feast honoring him.

The rains came, and the crops were planted. With the harvest, the people prepared the promised feast. Originally, wealthy land owners prepared the feast in the town square to feed the poor. Through the ages, those who have prayed for and been granted a favor express their thanks during this festivity that has come to be known as *la tavola di San Giuseppe*.

Saint Joseph is also the patron saint of the poor, the homeless and unwed mothers. Though the Saint Joseph's table by tradition should be open to everyone, tables in private homes can be limited to invited friends and family. The traditions, symbols, and menus are all very important to the feast, but may vary according to where in Sicily a family originated.

The tradition was brought to the United States in the late 19th and early 20th centuries by Sicilian immigrants who settled mostly in Louisiana, Texas, California, Colorado, New Jersey and New York. Saint Joseph's tables are very popular in New Orleans.

Symbols of the Feast

This is the Giordano altar. Note the lace cloth, votive candles, and bowl of fava beans.

One of the most important traditions is an altar to honor Saint Joseph. It should have three steps—a "stairway to heaven"—representing the Father, the Son, and the Holy Ghost. A large framed picture or statue of Saint Joseph should be the focal point centered on the altar. Lace tablecloths, representing the lace traditionally made by Sicilian mothers for their daughters' marriage trousseaus, should cover the buffet and the altar.

Although you will want to use your best china and crystal to honor *San Giuseppe*, the people of Sicily were generally very poor, so they would have set their buffet with affordable ceramic bowls handmade by Sicilian artisans. Silver bowls and platters would most likely not have been used. Votive candles should decorate all the tables; special Saint Joseph's day candles are available for purchase.

Dried fava beans should be displayed and distributed to guests. It is customary to provide guests with a small gift of bread to take home. My family usually makes small, brown-paper gift bags into which we put a few fava beans, a Saint Joseph's prayer card, a small roll, and an orange, which is a symbol of good health and prosperity.

Vases displaying wheat, a symbol of life, and spaghetti, representing food available with the end of the famine, should be placed on the altar. The use of floral arrangements is recommended. We make them plentiful at our table in anticipation of spring and rebirth. Lilies, representing purity, are traditionally associated with Saint Joseph because God made lilies spring forth from Joseph's staff.

Because Saint Joseph is also the patron saint of fruit vendors, fruits such as citrus, grapes, apples, pears, and figs that grow plentifully in Sicily should be displayed on the buffet as well as eaten. In fact, traditionally, only foods grown by the peasants or found growing wild were to be eaten during the feast. Many towns and villages in Sicily are fishing towns, or border water, and these towns always include fish in their feast. However, no meat is eaten at the feast. Even if the peasants could scrape together enough money to afford meat for their celebration, Saint Joseph's day occurs during Lent.

As a symbol of good luck as well as humility, lentils should be served in some form. It is also customary to serve them on New Year's Day to begin the year with luck.

The Saint Joseph's day bread is quite symbolic. Bread in Sicily is usually made with semolina and covered with sesame or poppy seeds. For the Saint Joseph's feast, breads are made into different shapes: bread shaped like a hook symbolizes the walking-staff (*bastone*) used by Joseph, which God made burst into bloom to prove to a nonbeliever that Joseph was a saint. The cross represents the death of Jesus, and bread shaped like a crown represents the thorns on Jesus' brow. Then there is my father's adaptation: a Star of David, symbolizing that Joseph was born Jewish, and both lived his life and was buried as a Jew.

As an inexpensive alternative to meat, egg dishes are always included in the feast. *Froggia*, frittatas, and omelets are all popular. Eggs represent fertility.

Pasta con sarde, which features a tomato sauce with fennel, sultana raisins, sardines, capers, garlic, and parsley, is the traditional pasta dish. It is garnished with toasted bread crumbs instead of grated cheese, because cheese was too expensive. The bread crumbs symbolize sacrifice and poverty. They also represent sawdust, a by-product of carpentry, which was the source of Joseph's livelihood.

Vegetable dishes should be served in abundance—hot or cold, pickled or marinated. Mushrooms, asparagus, cardoons, dandelions, escarole, spinach, fennel, arugula, artichokes, eggplant, tomatoes, peppers, beets—the list of possibilities is endless, and a number of traditional recipes for them are found on pages 48-67. Fennel, which grows wild in abundance in Sicily in the springtime, is considered to be both sacred and healing. Olives are called the fruit of the earth.

Sicilians regard fish and bread as gifts from God to his people. Commonly served are cod or *baccalá*, as well as shrimp, mussels, calamari, and smelt. Swordfish and tuna are also indigenous to Sicily.

The sweets offered often include *pignolatti, sfinge, cannoli, zeppole,* and cookies.

Special prayers and an explanation of the feast should precede the meal, and either the host or an honored guest may offer them.

Another form of ceremony is to have a "saints' table" decorated with fine china, crystal, and lace cloths. Guests are chosen to play the parts of Joseph, Mary, and Jesus, and "servants" are assigned to serve them first. Once the saints have been served, guests are invited to "taste" the foods displayed. A young child plays the part of Jesus, also representing the rebirth of nature in spring.

The miracle of the Swallows of Capistrano takes place each year at the Mission San Juan Capistano, on March 19th, Saint Joseph's Day. As the little birds wing their way back to the most famous Mission in California, the village of San Juan Capistrano takes on a festive air, and visitors from all over the world and all walks of life gather in great numbers to witness the miracle of the return of the swallows.

Each year the "scout swallows" precede the main flock by a few days. Their chief duty seems to be to clear the way for the main flock to arrive at the Old Mission of Capistrano. With the arrival of early dawn on Saint Joseph's Day, the little birds begin to arrive and start rebuilding their mud nests, which are clinging to the ruins of the old stone church of San Juan Capistrano. The arches of the two-story, vaulted chapel were left bare and exposed when the roof collapsed during the earthquake of 1812. This chapel, said to be the largest and most ornate of any of the missions, now has a more humble destiny-that of housing the birds that St. Francis loved so well.

After a summer spent within the sheltered walls of the Old Mission, the swallows take flight again. On the day of San Juan, October 23, they circle the Mission bidding farewell to the "Jewel of All Missions" and leave San Juan Capistrano for another year.

Order of Service

- Guests converge. A small appetizer can be served at this time.
- Tupa Tupa
- Prayer
- Blessing of the Table or Altar (by a Priest or Other Honored Guest)
- Mangia! (Eat!)

"Tupa Tupa"
Knocking for Saint Joseph's day

Some families add to their Saint Joseph's day festivities the tradition of "Tupa Tupa," which represents the Holy Family's search for food and shelter. Tupa Tupa involves picking players to represent the Holy Family and angels, who proceed to knock on three doors in search of food and shelter. At the first two doors, someone inside asks, "Who is there?"

The response is: "Jesus, Mary, and Joseph."

The following dialogue then takes place:
"What do you want?"
"We seek food and shelter"
"There is no room for you here."

When the family arrives at the third door, which is the house hosting the Saint Joseph's table, the response is: "Welcome to this house! The table is set; the food is prepared. Come in and honor us with your presence!"

The saints are then seated and served. When they have finished their meal, the guests are welcomed and served with love and warm hospitality in imitation of Saint Joseph.

Source: Viva San Guiseppe: A Guide for St. Joseph Altars

A Prayer for the Saint Joseph's Day Meal

Before beginning the meal, gather guests around the buffet. Elect a spokesman or a small group and give each a part. Explain the following: why there is a table, the history of the holiday, some of the symbols that are used, your menu. Then recite a Saint Joseph's prayer (see pages 9-10).

Judge Joseph Matina and Marian Giordano blessing the table.

Saint Joseph…we ask your intercession for all our intentions.
Saint Joseph the Worker, Patron Saint of the little man,
the poor - new and old,
the unemployed and those with freedom stifled.
We honor you once a year with our fish and orange
also with our prayers.
And we pray now, more than ever before, that those who
are in need will have their needs
fulfilled, but through our efforts and human miracles.

VIVA SAN GIUSEPPE!

Honoring of Saint Joseph by having a table such as this is a tradition long celebrated in Sicily. It began in 1282 when the French soldiers came into a Sicilian Village and created a great disturbance. In retaliation, the village killed many of the French soldiers. Soon after, there was a great drought. This was interpreted as a sign from God as punishment for the killings. To make amends with the Lord, the people asked Saint Joseph to intercede for them with a promise to plant grain enough to feed the entire village.

Throughout the years, the tradition has grown and varied. People added their own intentions. The foods vary somewhat, but the table is always a meatless meal. We hope you enjoy our special table.

VIVA SAN GIUSEPPE!

Many Sicilians believe the legend in this prayer to be true; however, this story is actually a simplification of the Sicilian Vespers, which have nothing to do with the drought or Saint Joseph's day. Sicilians did rebel in 1288, ending French rule there.

This prayer is from the family of Sylvia Fredericks who has held many of her own tables in her home in Eggertsville, New York.

Blessing of the Table and Altar

Now, let us call upon Joseph, Patron of this table and Protector of the poor, and ask him to guide us in God's ways and to keep us from all selfishness:

Leader:	From being selfish and possessive,
All:	Protect us, Saint Joseph
Leader:	From ignoring the hungry and homeless,
All:	Protect us, Saint Joseph
Leader:	From neglecting the elderly and poor,
All:	Protect us, Saint Joseph
Leader:	From wasting the good things of the earth,
All:	Protect us, Saint Joseph.

PRAYER

Leader:	Because you cared for Mary and Jesus, we pray:
All:	Viva San Giuseppe!!!
Leader:	Because you teach us to care for others, we say:
All:	Viva San Giuseppe!!!
Leader:	Because you protect us from sin and selfishness, we shout:
All:	VIVA SAN GIUSEPPE!!!

Buon appetito!
Please taste from our table and enjoy the meal.

When hosting a Saint Joseph's celebration, it is customary to place an olive branch above your door to let people know they are welcome and that a table is being held.

The Saint Joseph's Pantry and Glossary

Ammudicata
Breadcrumbs

Basil
Fresh basil is a versatile herb—easy to grow and easy to use. It can be used raw in a salad or cooked in a recipe. When cooking with basil, be sure to add it at the end of the cooking process. It is preferable to chiffonade basil than to chop it (see chiffonade below).

Burdocks/Cardoons
Burdocks grow wild and are smaller and tenderer. Cardoons are domestic, sold in stores and are larger and easier to work with. Both are akin to artichokes and resemble them in flavor.

Cheese
Cheese is not traditionally served at the Saint Joseph's table. However, here cheese is included in some recipes where it enhances the dish. If you are preparing these dishes for Saint Joseph's day, you may choose to omit it to adhere more closely to tradition.

Chiffonade
Using a sharp knife, slice through the herb in small, julienne strips so as not to bruise the leaves.

Cippolini
Pronounced chip-oh-LEE-nee, this is a smaller, flat, pale onion. The flesh is slightly yellowish in color and the skins are thin and papery. The color of the skin ranges from pale yellow to the light brown color of Spanish onions. *Cippolini* have more residual sugar than garden-variety white or yellow onions, making them sweeter, but not as sweet as shallots.

Eggs
Assume that recipes call for extra-large eggs, and, when possible, use them at room temperature.

Erba mari
Wild bitter greens.

Ditalini
Pasta shaped like little fingers.

Garlic

In our family we use garlic sparingly, always making sure that it is fresh. You might consider only cracking a clove, adding it to a dish for a while and removing it before serving.

Gremolata or Gremolada

A chopped herb condiment typically made of lemon zest, garlic, and parsley. It is a traditional accompaniment to the Milanese braised veal shank dish ossobuco alla milanese.

Kitchen-cut

Chunky style canned tomato in juice.

Maccu

A thick bean soup.

Minestra

Sicilian for soup. Minestre is the plural form.

Minestrone

The Big Soup.

Mint

Fresh mint is a wonderful herb. Once you plant it, it will grow like a weed in your garden, returning annually and spreading if you don't contain it!

Olive Oil

Use 100% olive oil or extra virgin olive oil. I use 100% olive oil for cooking and extra virgin olive oil for salads and cold dishes. Pomace olive oil, which comes from the third pressing of the olives, is not good and should not be used. The good flavor is in the first pressing for extra virgin and the second pressing for 100%. In Italy and Sicily extra virgin olive oil is used for every thing, including frying. The rest is exported to the U.S.

Panelle

Sicilian street food, of Arab origin, from Palermo, made with chick pea flour.

Parsley

Use Italian flat leaf parsley, which is more flavorful than curly parsley.

Perciatelli

Long, hollow pasta rods, thicker than spaghetti.

Pignolatti
Small balls of fried dough, glazed with honey and stacked in the shape of a pine cone. Also known as honeyed pinecone.

Salt
Unless I am baking, I almost always use kosher salt. Sea salt is also fine and is used quite frequently in Sicilian cooking because it is a natural product of Trapani, the capital of Trapani Province on the west coast of Sicily. The unrefined mineral-rich crystals are prized for their sharp intensity of flavor. The salt is produced by natural evaporation, a product of the wind, the sun, and the sea.

Sfinge
Fried dough, crème puff, or pate a choux sometimes filled with crème or ricotta cheese.

Shortening
Traditionally, the shortening used in any recipe in this book would have been lard. Today, for health reasons, lard is seldom used. Crisco shortening, margarine, butter, or light variations of these are all acceptable, although results will vary slightly from product to product.

Stock
Since tradition dictates that this be a meatless meal, vegetable stock is preferable to chicken stock. Don't worry about making your own. Sicilians are known for using boullion cubes to flavor their soups and sauces.

Tallegio
A strong, ripe, creamy Italian cheese.

Temperature
Many dishes in this book recommend serving dishes at room temperature rather than chilled. This is not a matter of convenience; the flavors of foods at room temperature are enhanced and heightened.

Tomatoes
In many parts of the country, home-grown tomatoes may not be available in March. But with today's hothouse growing methods, you can still get a decent tomato out of season. This is where you must spend a little more money. Buy either the vine-ripened hothouse tomatoes (with the vine still attached) or Roma tomatoes. I never decide until I look at the tomatoes in the store. Buy the deepest red, best-smelling, firmest tomatoes available.

Zeppole
Fried dough, crème puff, or pate a choux dessert, sometimes filled with crème, ricotta cheese or jelly.

Zuppa
An Italian soup or stew. Zuppe is the plural form.

Sicilian Dialects

Webster's Dictionary defines a dialect as "a regional variety of language distinguished by features of vocabulary, grammar and pronunciation from other varieties and constituting together with them a single language."

Sicilian is a dialect of the Italian language, but there are at least a dozen different Sicilian dialects in the towns and villages of Sicily, some of them very distinctive. It is not uncommon for Sicilians from different villages to have difficulty understanding one another. This broad range of dialects stems from Sicily's long history of invasions. Just as the culinary landscape has been affected by conquering armies from different lands, so has its language. Mainly comprised of Arab and Greek influences, Sicilian language is also influenced by linguistic elements of the Norman French, Spanish, and Catalan languages, to name a few.

Thus the inconsistencies in spelling found in this cookbook, and spellings that differ from other Sicilian or Italian cookbooks, are because I have collected authentic recipes for decades from different families and different regions of Sicily. In addition, many immigrants, like my grandmother, emigrated at an early age with little education. Possible misspellings compound the difference in dialects. In fact, this also impacts my spelling when I write up Daily Specials! Every effort has been made to use the most common form of words in recipes and to be consistent throughout, but sometimes it's more important to honor traditional spelling.

Some examples of these regional variations include: Fennel can be called either finocchi or finocchio. An omelet is equally well known as a froscia (plural: froscie), a frittata or a froggia. Garbanzo beans, which have a variety of names in English-consider chick peas and chi chi beans-are called both ci ci ri and chi chi ri. A generic word for soup is minestra (plural: minestre) which becomes minestrone, the Big Soup. But soup in Italian is also zuppa (plural: zuppe). Those fabulous fig cookies can be spelled cucidati or cucciddati, and I have recipes for honeyed pine cones that use both pignolatti and pignocatta.

Whatever the spelling or usage, the food and its flavors provide a common language that overcomes all linguistic idiosyncrasies. Buon appetito!

Antipasti/Appetizers

Caponata

Ci ci ri (Chickpea Dip)

Roasted Eggplant Dip

Stuffed Eggs

Fava Beans with Pecorino

Fig-Walnut Tapenade

Panelle (Chickpea Pancakes)

Pistachio–Orange Tapenade

*Antipasti/*Appetizers

Sicilians are not big fans of appetizers. A few cold cuts, a wedge of cheese, some crusty bread, some pickled peppers, and a spread or two on a special occasion are more than enough. For Saint Joseph's day, you may wish to put out just a few tidbits so your guests can nibble while the group assembles and you finish your table. But don't overdo the antipasti; keep them hungry for the main event.

Tapenade • Caponata • Ci ci ri

Caponata

1/4 cup olive oil
2 eggplants, peeled and diced in 1/2-inch cubes
1 medium onion, finely chopped
2 red peppers, diced in 1/2-inch cubes
2 green peppers, diced in 1/2-inch cubes
4 stalks celery, diced
4 Roma tomatoes, diced
1 cup fresh tomato sauce or canned tomatoes with juices
1 cup golden raisins
1/2 cup pine nuts, toasted
1/4 cup red wine vinegar
1/4 cup capers, drained
1/2 cup Sicilian green olives, diced
1/4 cup fresh mint, chopped
1/4 cup fresh basil, chiffonade
1 bunch Italian parsley, chopped

Heat the oil in a large, heavy pot over medium heat. Add the eggplant, onion, peppers, and celery. Sauté until vegetables are hot and coated with oil. Add the tomatoes, tomato sauce, raisins, pine nuts (reserving some for garnish), vinegar, capers, and olives. Cover and simmer for about 12 minutes until eggplant and onion are tender, stirring occasionally. Mix in the mint, basil, and parsley. Transfer the caponata to a serving bowl. Sprinkle with toasted pine nuts. Serve warm, at room temperature, or cold.

Caponata is a traditional Sicilian vegetable dip usually served as an appetizer with bread. It is sweet and sour, fresh and tasty. I enjoy making it at the end of summer with fresh produce and canning it to serve on Saint Joseph's day. It can be served at room temperature or warm as an appetizer while your guests are gathering before the meal or as one of the vegetable dishes. If you don't have any stored in your pantry from the summer harvest, you can make it two or three days in advance. Just cover and chill.

Ci ci ri (Chickpea Dip)

2 cans chickpeas, drained and rinsed
4 cloves garlic, chopped
1/2 cup olive oil
1/2 cup lemon juice
1/2 cup chopped Italian parsley
1/2 cup chopped scallions
Kosher salt
Pepper

Combine all ingredients in a food processor, pulsing to a chunky consistency. Add salt and pepper to taste. Serve with grilled bread.

During the Sicilian Vespers, Sicilians massacred the French who were ruling in Sicily at the time. The Sicilians would use the word "ci ci ri" (pronounced che-che-re) to find imposters trying to infiltrate their forces. The French, of course, could not pronounce the word like the Sicilians did, and were exposed.

Roasted Eggplant Dip

Preheat oven to 350°F.

4 eggplants, halved
1/4 cup lemon juice
1/4 cup olive oil
2 cloves garlic, minced
1/4 cup chopped Italian parsley
1/4 cup minced scallions
Kosher salt
Black pepper

Rub the eggplant with oil, salt, and pepper. Place on a baking sheet cut side down and roast at 350°F for 25 to 30 minutes, until soft. Scrape out the majority of seeds and discard. Scoop out the eggplant with a spoon and combine with other ingredients in the food processor. Process until mixture is puréed.

Stuffed Eggs

Hard-boiled eggs stuffed with Italian tuna, capers, and olive oil drizzle.

12 eggs, hard boiled
1 can Italian tuna, packed in oil, drained
1 tablespoon capers
Extra virgin olive oil

Cool and peel the hard-boiled eggs, and cut them in half lengthwise. Remove the yolks and mix with the drained tuna and capers. Stuff the egg whites with the mixture and drizzle with olive oil.

> An easy and convenient way to hard-boil eggs is to place them in a pot, cover them with cold water, and when the water comes to a rapid boil, cover the pot, turn off the heat, and allow the eggs to rest for 10 minutes. Cool the eggs under cold running water and peel immediately.

Fava Beans with *Pecorino*

To prepare a spring bounty of fresh fava beans, simply remove the beans from the pods and blanch in boiling salted water until the outer skin pops off. Serve the beans cold with shaved curls of an aged sharp pecorino cheese.

Fig–Walnut *Tapenade*

1 8-ounce package dried figs
1 cup walnuts, toasted
1/2 cup sugar
1/2 cup olive oil
1 tablespoon balsamic vinegar

> Crostini is simply bread that is sliced, rubbed with olive oil and garlic, and grilled. Use it as a vehicle for spreads and toppings.

Note: Place figs in hot water for 5 minutes to rehydrate. Drain. Combine all ingredients in a food processor and pulse until blended. Serve on crostini.

Panelle (Chickpea Pancakes)

A delicious traditional street snack of Arab origin from Palermo.

2 cups chickpea flour
1 tablespoon salt
4 cups water, lightly salted
2 tablespoons parsley, minced

2 tablespoons lemon juice
Soybean oil for frying
Lemon wedges
Kosher salt

Stir the flour into the water over moderate heat, mixing steadily in the same direction with a wooden spoon until a soft, lump-free paste forms. Add the parsley. When the paste begins to pull away from the sides of the pot, turn it out onto an oiled wooden cutting board. Spread the paste to about a 1/4-inch thickness. Once the paste has cooled, cut it into 1-inch by 3-inch rectangles and fry in hot oil. Arrange the rectangles on a serving plate and sprinkle with the juice. Garnish with lemon wedges for squeezing. Season with kosher salt.

Pistachio–Orange *Tapenade*

This traditional Sicilian topping can be served on crostini as an antipasto
or used as a topping for fish.

1 cup pistachios, shelled
1 teaspoon orange zest
1/3 cup orange juice
1 tablespoon lemon juice

1/2 cup extra virgin olive oil
1/2 cup ammudicata (see page 24)
2 cloves garlic, chopped
1 teaspoon kosher salt

Chop the pistachios in a food processor. Add all the other ingredients except the oil and turn on the food processor. Drizzle the oil in a slow steady stream. Scape down food processor with a spatula and make sure everything is well blended. Store in refrigerator for about a week.

Pane/Bread

Ammudicata (Bread Crumbs)

Foccacia

Mama Dano's Bread

Pane di San Giuseppe

Semolina Bread

Pane/Bread

Bread is a favorite food in Sicily, and it is found on the table at every meal. Sitting down to dinner without fresh bread of some sort on the table is unthinkable. I remember meals in my childhood that were wonderful and very filling, my grandmother encouraging us to eat second or third helpings. When we answered, "Oh, no thank you, Grandma, everything was wonderful, but I'm so full!" her reply (with a smile, a hearty laugh, and a wave of her hand) would always be, "Eh, eat it without bread." As an adult I have come to understand this to mean that without bread you can never be full. But it was always said as though it were a private joke. I'm still not sure I get it.

When Grandma made bread, I was always excited. There was no taste as good as her bread right out of the oven with just a little olive oil and salt. Mmmmmnn! I'm lucky enough to have inherited her two cream-colored earthenware ceramic bread bowls, with one thick rust-colored stripe and two thin green stripes. I use them for my dough to rise in and for making pickles, nothing else. Except for the age cracks on the inside of the pottery, they still look brand new.

Ammudicata (Bread Crumbs)

Preheat oven to 350°F.

During the Saint Joseph's day feast, toasted bread crumbs are used to replace grated cheese. They symbolize the deprivation that led to the celebration, the drought that caused everything to be dry. Also, Joseph was a carpenter, and the bread crumbs symbolize the sawdust produced by his labors.

Despite the symbolism, bread crumbs don't have to-and shouldn't-taste like sawdust! Start with a good quality Italian bread (a few days old is fine). Rip it into small chunks, drizzle it with extra virgin olive oil and melted butter, and sprinkle with salt and pepper. Toast at 350°F until golden brown. Allow to cool. Place the bread in a food processor and chop until it is finely ground. Just before serving, blend in a little chopped Italian parsley. Serve in a pretty little bowl next to the pasta.

Foccacia

Preheat oven to 400°F.

Bread dough
Corn meal
Olive oil
Crushed red pepper

Garlic, chopped
Rosemary, chopped
Romano cheese, grated

Prepare Mama Dano's bread dough recipe (see opposite page). Divide the dough into 8 pieces* and roll each out to fit on a greased and cornmeal-rubbed 12-inch round tray. Cover and allow to rise to about 1-1/2 to 2 inches. Rub with olive oil, pepper, garlic, rosemary and cheese. Bake at 400°F for 15 minutes or until golden brown.

*Note: Freeze some dough if you like, or make bread with it.

Mama Dano's Bread

Preheat oven to 400°F.

6 loaves
1 cup water
2 packs compressed dry yeast
1 teaspoon sugar
10 pounds flour (unbleached King Arthur)
7 rounded tablespoons salt
6 cups lukewarm water
1-1/2 sticks margarine (soft) or lard
7 tablespoons sugar
Egg for brushing loaves
Sesame seeds

3 loaves
1 cup water
2 packs compressed dry yeast
1 teaspoon sugar
10 cups flour (unbleached King Arthur)
3 tablespoons salt
3 cups lukewarm water (not including yeast mix)
¾ stick Crisco shortening
7 tablespoons sugar
Egg for brushing loaves
Sesame seeds

To proof the yeast, place the first three ingredients in a small metal bowl over the glow of the pilot light. Stir and let stand until the mixture foams.

Put the flour and the salt in large mixing bowl, mix, and make a well in the middle. Pour in the water, margarine, sugar, and yeast mixture, and gradually mix with a wooden spoon. Knead for 8 to 10 minutes until no more flour is taken up, and the dough is smooth and elastic. Place the dough in a clean ceramic bowl and rub butter on its sides. Cover the bowl with a dry cloth and let the dough rise for 2 hours. Knead the dough again for 1 to 2 minutes. Let rise 1 more hour. Cut the dough into 3 or 6 loaves. Place on baking sheets or in loaf pans. Let rise another hour. Optional: Brush the loaves with whole beaten egg and sprinkle with sesame seeds. Bake at 400°F for 10 minutes. Reduce oven to 350°F and continue baking for 20 to 25 more minutes.

Note:
If you like, you can mix the dough in a mixer. Put the flour and salt in first and mix briefly. Add the shortening, sugar, proofed yeast mix, and blend on low, gradually adding water. When blended, turn to a higher speed, kneading for 2 to 3 minutes. For a thicker crust, use a spray bottle to spray cold water into the oven, over the crust while baking. Spray once or twice during baking, at 10 minutes and 15 minutes into the baking time.

Pane di San Giuseppe

Preheat oven to 350°F.

This bread, called *Pane di San Giuseppe*, is traditionally made for the Feast of Saint Joseph. This is not the bread we serve in our house, but it is a traditional variation. I did serve it once several years ago, and it was wonderful, very different and quite beautiful.

2 to 3 cups unbleached flour
1 package active dry yeast
1 tablespoon honey
2/3 cup hot water
1/2 teaspoon salt

2 tablespoons butter
3 tablespoons anise seed
1/3 cup golden raisins
Cornmeal

Combine 1-1/2 cups of the flour and the yeast, honey, water, salt, butter, and anise in a large bowl. Mix thoroughly. Add the raisins. Continue mixing, adding flour until the dough begins to pull away from the sides of the bowl. Turn the dough out onto a lightly floured surface. Knead for 8 to 10 minutes, until the dough is smooth and elastic, adding flour as necessary to prevent stickiness. Lightly oil a large bowl. Place the dough in the bowl and turn to coat on all sides. Cover with plastic wrap and place in a warm, draft-free place until doubled in bulk, about 1 hour.

Grease a baking sheet and sprinkle with cornmeal. Punch down the dough. Shape into a long loaf. Place the loaf on the baking sheet and make three or four 1/2-inch diagonal slashes on the top. Cover with a tea towel and let dough rise until doubled in bulk, about 30 minutes.

Traditionally, the bread is shaped to look like a patriarch's beard by making five torpedo loaves of graduated lengths: 1 long, 2 medium, and 2 short. Place the loaves close together on a baking sheet in the following order: 1 short, 1 medium, 1 long, 1 medium, 1 short. They will rise together, and you'll have *Pane di San Giuseppe*.

Mist loaves with water or white vinegar before, and twice during, baking. Bake at 350°F for about 40 minutes. Transfer to a wire rack to cool.

Semolina Bread

Preheat oven to 375°F.

1 cup warm water
2 cakes compressed yeast or 2 packages
  dry yeast
1 teaspoon sugar
4 cups semolina flour
6 cups unbleached flour

2 tablespoons salt
4 to 4-1/2 cups warm water
5 tablespoons olive oil
1 tablespoon sugar
1/4 cup sesame seeds

To proof the yeast, stir together the cup of water, 2 packages of yeast, and teaspoon of sugar in a bowl. Let stand until it foams.

Put the semolina flour and 5 cups of the unbleached flour in a large ceramic bowl, mix in the salt, and make a well in the center. Pour three cups of water and the yeast mix into the well. Begin working the dough with a wooden spoon, slowly incorporating flour from the sides. As the dough begins to thicken use your hands to mix it. Once the water is absorbed, start kneading the dough, adding more water, little by little as needed. Unlike other bread doughs, semolina bread dough should be sticky and moist. Knead the dough for about 20 minutes-or until your arms feel ready to fall off-folding the dough in half and pushing down, over and over again. Use the last cup of flour as needed while kneading the dough on the counter. Add

2 to 3 tablespoons of the oil when done kneading. When the dough is smooth and elastic, it is ready. Cut the dough into four pieces.

Lightly sprinkle two baking pans with semolina flour. Form the loaves into the shapes that you would like. Place loaves on the baking pans. Brush the tops with the remaining oil and sprinkle with the seeds. Cover with a clean cloth and put in a warm place to double in size, 45 to 60 minutes. Bake the loaves at 375°F for 50 minutes to an hour. Loaves are done when they turn golden brown and start to crack on top.

Uova/Eggs

Spinach *Frittata*

Mushroom and Asparagus *Frittata*

Cauliflower *Froggia (Froscia)*

Quiche

Pickled Eggs

Uova/Eggs

Eggs are an integral component of Sicilian cooking. Meat was not always an option for the island's poor peasants. Eggs, representing fertility, were an inexpensive alternative and a good source of protein. Egg dishes are always included in the Saint Joseph's day feast.

I recall the first time Grandma Josephine "snuck" hard-boiled eggs into my spaghetti with meatballs. I was shocked! She laughed and told me that when people had no money to buy meat, they would pretend the eggs were meatballs. I was skeptical, but my father always urged me to be a pioneer, to try new things, so I did. They were wonderful, and I always try to include them in my table.

I consider a *frittata* a baked egg dish, like a casserole, while a *froggia* is made in a

pan on the stove, like an unfolded omelet. Some will say that a *frittata* is just an Italian omelet, since *frittata* means fried. I believe this is a regional interpretation. The baked *frittata* would simply be a variation. In Sicilian, *froscia* is the word for omelet (plural: *froscia*). In this book, I use the term *froggia* that my family inherited from my grandmother as the word for omelet. It appears to be merely a slight variation of the Sicilian term, and I am reluctant to remove it. Both are wonderful if cooked correctly. *Froscia* need a little more hands-on prep time, but are less likely to overcook. They are also easier to time because they take only minutes. On the other hand, a *frittata* gets mixed and placed in the oven and can then be put on the table hot, if timed correctly, with dinner.

Spinach *Frittata*

Preheat oven to 300°F.

2 large leeks
Olive oil for sautéing
2 pounds spinach
20 extra-large eggs
2 cups heavy cream
2 tablespoons kosher salt
Cracked pepper
1 teaspoon nutmeg
2 cups diced Roma tomatoes
2 tablespoons fresh basil, chiffonade

To prepare the leeks, slice them down the middle and into 1/2-inch half moons. Wash two or three times in cold water. Sauté the leeks in the oil until wilted. Blanch the spinach, cool under cold water, and drain.

Whisk the eggs well with the cream. Season the mixture with salt, pepper, and nutmeg. Grease a 9-inch by 9-inch (or 8-inch by 10-inch) casserole or baking dish. Pour in the egg mixture, layer in the leeks, tomatoes, spinach, and basil, and bake covered for 30 minutes. Uncover and continue baking for an additional 40 minutes. Serve warm.

Note: For a buffet, I recommend prepping the vegetables a day ahead and assembling the frittata and other egg dishes as day-of projects. Cook these dishes right before company is due to arrive, remove them from the oven, and cover with foil to keep warm. Then, right before or after you cook your fish, put it back in the oven for 10 minutes to serve hot.

Mushroom and Asparagus *Frittata*

2 large onions, caramelized
Butter for sautéing
2 tablespoons balsamic vinegar
1 pound asparagus
1 pound wild mushrooms (cremini, portabello, shiitake)
Olive oil for sautéing
20 eggs
2 cups heavy cream
1 teaspoon nutmeg
2 tablespoons kosher salt
Pepper
2 tablespoons fresh thyme

To caramelize the onions, sauté them in butter in a cast iron pan on medium heat until very soft, stirring often. Add balsamic vinegar and continue cooking the onions uncovered, reducing the mix until syrupy and caramelized.

Place the asparagus in boiling water for 4 minutes to blanch, then shock by plunging into ice water. Sauté the mushrooms in oil until wilted. Whisk the eggs well with the cream. Season with salt, pepper, and nutmeg. Grease a 9-inch by 9-inch (or 8-inch by 10-inch) casserole or baking dish. Pour the egg mix into the dish, layer in the mushrooms, asparagus, and thyme. Bake covered at 300°F for 30 minutes. Uncover and continue baking for an additional 40 minutes. Serve warm.

Cauliflower *Froggia (Froscia)*

8 large eggs
1/2 cup fresh basil, chiffonade (optional)
1/2 teaspoon dried oregano (optional)
Salt
Pepper

2 tablespoons butter (1/4 stick)
2 tablespoons olive oil
3 scallions, chopped
1 to 2 cups cauliflower, blanched and chopped

Beat the eggs lightly. Add the herbs and salt and pepper to taste. Melt the butter and olive oil in a 10- to 12-inch nonstick skillet on medium heat. Sauté the scallions briefly. When the pan is hot but not smoking, add the egg mixture. Cover and cook for 1 to 2 minutes or until edges start cooking. Using a wooden spoon, gently push eggs from the edge of the pan toward the middle, letting uncooked egg mixture fill in behind the spoon. Repeat 4 or 5 times. Add the vegetables. Cover and continue cooking for 1 to 2 minutes. Gently loosen the omelet from the bottom of the pan, place an inverted plate over the pan and flip onto the plate. Slide the omelette back into the pan for 1 to 2 more minutes to cook the bottom. Eggs should be slightly loose; do not overcook. Slide omlette back onto the plate. Allow to cool and cut with a sharp knife. Serve at room temperature.

Note: For an 8-egg froggia, add 2 cups of the filling of your choice. If the filling should be cooked, do so before putting it in the froggia. Blanch broccoli, asparagus, dandelions or rapini, sauté mushrooms. Use some type of onion or garlic for flavor (leeks, shallots, red onion, Vidalia onions). Sweat the onions in a pan so they are cooked. Finish the flavor profile of the froggia by choosing a fresh or dried herb that complements the dish.

Suggested filling combinations:

Mushroom-leek-thyme
Cauliflower-scallion-oregano
Asparagus-shallots-dill

Rapini-red onion-tomato
Vidalia onion-tomato-basil
Peppers-onions-oregano

Quiche

Preheat oven to 300°F.

Quiche is actually a French dish, but it goes well on the Saint Joseph's table because you can serve a quiche warm or at room temperature. Vary the ingredients using Sicilian vegetables that are traditional for the feast. If you plan to make three or four pie pans of quiche, using a variety of fillings is a nice touch. Cauliflower and green onion, mushroom and spinach, dandelion greens and sundried tomatoes, all work well. Use any combination you like, but remember to use no meat or cheese (unless you want to cheat...)

Vinegar pie crust - Makes one 9-inch crust

1-1/2 cups unbleached all-purpose flour
1/4 teaspoon salt
1/4 teaspoon baking powder
4 tablespoons butter, cut in 1/2-inch cubes

1/4 cup vegetable shortening
1 teaspoon white vinegar
3-5 tablespoons ice water

In a medium-sized mixing bowl, combine the flour, salt, and baking powder. Using your fingers or a fork, cut in the butter and shortening, to produce pea-size lumps. Mix the vinegar with 3 tablespoons of the water. Sprinkle over flour mixture, and mix with a fork. Using your hands, pack the dough. If it doesn't stick together add the additional 1-2 tablespoons of water. Shape the dough into a ball, wrap in plastic wrap and refrigerate for at least 30 minutes before rolling.

Filling

12 eggs
2 cups heavy cream
1 teaspoon nutmeg
Salt

Pepper
2 cups vegetable filling (of your choice)
2 tablespoons fresh herbs or 1 teaspoon dried
  herbs (of your choice)

Roll out the dough to fit your pan. Place vegetable and herb filling in the shell. Mix the eggs, cream, nutmeg, and herbs. Add salt and pepper to taste. Pour the egg mixture over the filling. Bake at 300°F for 1 hour. Insert a toothpick to test for doneness; if it is not dry, cook a bit more. If the top is browning but the eggs are not cooked through, cover with foil for the last few minutes in the oven.

Pickled Eggs

These are just plain fun! Pickled in beet brine, the eggs become a beautiful beet red. Prepare the pickled beet recipe on page 52. Once the beets have marinated, steal some of the beet juice from the container and put peeled, hard-boiled eggs into the liquid (see recipe for perfect hard-boiled eggs on page 20). You can prepare the beets and the pickled eggs a week before the party.

Note: If you don't want the eggs red, but like a little spice, use the brine from the Pickled Pepper recipe on page 54 instead!

Insalata/Salad

Arugula, Fennel and Avocado Salad

Marinated Artichoke Salad

Asparagus, Red Pepper and Fava Salad

Chi Chi Bean Salad

Dandelion Greens Salad

Escarole Greens Salad

Insalata di Finocchi (Fennel Salad)

Fennel, Orange and Olive Salad

Schiacciate (Marinated Olive Salad)

Sicilian Potato Salad

Tomato, Onion and Mint Salad

Roasted Red Pepper Salad

Insalata/Salad

In my family, when you eat dinner at home, there is always a dinner salad on the table. It is not always the same, but it usually has most of the same components. The salad should be dressed at the table just before eating. The greens should be the very best quality available at the grocery store. Romaine is a staple, and radicchio is always welcome. If the romaine doesn't look good, you can substitute some Boston bibb, escarole, or endive. Tomatoes, cucumbers, and red onion are the norm. Try Roma or grape tomatoes. I used to say "never eat tomatoes out of season," but today you can usually get a good "vine ripe," Roma, or grape tomato if you're willing to pay a little more. Midwinter, if you need a flavor boost for your tomatoes, toss them in a little olive oil, salt, and pepper. Cucumbers have a tendency to be very fat and tasteless out of season. Try English cucumbers instead. They last longer in the refrigerator, have fewer seeds (so they're "burpless"), and have good flavor. Black olives, chickpeas, celery, and cheeses (except for your Saint Joseph's table!) are all wonderful ingredients as well.

Arugula, Fennel and Avocado Salad

1 fennel bulb, shaved thin
Juice of 1 lemon
Salt
Pepper
3 oranges, peeled
2 avocados
1 red onion, shaved
12 ounces arugula, washed and drained
Orange vinaigrette

Toss the fennel with some of the lemon juice, salt, and pepper. Remove the white skin from the oranges with a paring knife and slice them crosswise into 1/4-inch slices. Slice the avocado into wedges and toss with the remaining lemon juice. Shave as much of the red onion as desired. Make orange vinaigrette. Assemble the salad ingredients and dress at the table.

Orange Vinaigrette
1 6-ounce can orange juice concentrate
1 ounce tequila
1/4 cup honey
1 ounce grenadine
2 teaspoons chili powder
2 cups olive oil
1 teaspoon garlic
Salt
Pepper

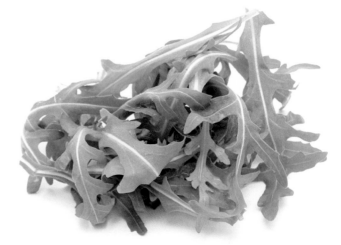

Combine all ingredients except the oil in a bowl. Whisk in the oil in a slow, steady stream to form an emulsion. Add up to a 1/2 cup of water to adjust consistency. Season to taste with salt and pepper.

Marinated Artichoke Salad

2 14-ounce cans quartered artichokes
  (water packed)
1/2 red onion, slivered
3 stalks celery, sliced
2 tablespoons chopped Italian parsley

2 tablespoons fresh basil, chiffonade
1 teaspoon dried oregano
1/2 cup extra virgin olive oil
1/4 cup red wine vinegar

Combine all ingredients and chill.

Asparagus, Red Pepper and Fava Salad

Preheat oven to 350°F.

4 red peppers, charred
2 pounds asparagus, trimmed and blanched
1 16-ounce can fava beans, drained
1/2 red onion, thinly sliced
1/2 cup extra virgin olive oil
Salt and pepper

Note: To char the peppers, use the "Roasted Red Pepper Salad" recipe on page 47. Peel the peppers, remove seeds and cut in strips. Trim the asparagus and snap off the ends where they break naturally. Blanch the asparagus in boiling water for 4 minutes and immediately cool under cold, running water to halt cooking.

Individually toss the asparagus, then the red peppers, then the fava beans with olive oil and salt and pepper to taste. Lay the asparagus in an oven-proof casserole, facing in the same direction. Place the red peppers in a line across the asparagus, below the tips of the asparagus. Place the fava beans in another line across the asparagus, after the red peppers, so you can see a strip of green, then red, then brown. Garnish with red onion. Bake for 15 minutes.

Chi Chi Bean Salad

2 14-ounce cans chi chi beans, drained and rinsed
1 red pepper, diced
1/2 red onion, diced
2 scallions, thinly sliced
1/4 cup chopped Italian parsley
1/4 cup chopped fresh mint
1 clove garlic, chopped
1/4 cup red wine vinegar
1/2 cup extra virgin olive oil
Salt
Pepper

Combine all the ingredients and chill. This salad can be made several days in advance.

Washing Greens

Greens need to be clean, cold, and crisp. Follow these instructions for washing all your greens, even if you are cooking them.
Break greens apart gently with your fingers. Wash greens well by immersing in cold water, agitating, and then pulling the greens out of the water. Do not just drain the water, as the dirt will fall right back onto the leaves. Rinse a second and even a third time, if needed, until the water appears clear.
Drain the greens well using a salad spinner or by patting dry.

Dandelion Greens Salad

2 bunches dandelion greens, washed
2 cloves garlic, smashed
4 anchovies
Juice of 2 lemons

2 tablespoons grated Parmesan
Freshly ground pepper
1 cup extra virgin olive oil

Trim and cut or tear dandelion greens to salad-size pieces. Add the garlic to the anchovies and mash together in the bottom of a wooden bowl. Add the lemon juice and Parmesan. Add the oil in a slow, steady stream while whisking to form an emulsion. Add the greens, tossing thoroughly with the dressing.

Escarole Greens Salad

1 head escarole greens, washed
Zest and juice of 1 lemon
Zest and juice of 1 lime
Zest and juice of 1 orange
1/2 cup white wine vinegar

1 shallot, minced
1 cup extra virgin olive oil
Salt
Pepper

Tear the escarole into salad-size pieces. Combine the zest and juice and vinegar in a bowl with the shallot. Add the oil in a slow steady stream to form an emulsion. Toss greens with enough dressing to coat the greens and serve.

Note: Serve side-by-side with the Fennel, Orange, and Olive Salad on page 43 for a beautiful presentation.

Insalata di Finocchi (Fennel Salad)

This salad presents fennel in its simplest form, the flavors highlighted with lemon, olive oil, salt and pepper.

2 to 4 bulbs fennel, quartered and sliced thin
Extra virgin olive oil
Fresh lemon juice (1-2 lemons)
Salt
Pepper

Toss the fennel with the oil and lemon juice to coat. Season with salt and pepper. Serve immediately.

Grilled Fennel

Grilling gives fennel a wonderful smoky flavor. Simply quarter the fennel bulbs and slice each quarter once more, or slice the fennel in 1/2-inch slices. Toss with olive oil, salt and pepper. Grill on medium-hot grill until tender and slightly charred.

Fennel, Orange and Olive Salad

This is the classic Saint Joseph's day salad. Beautiful, flavorful, and oh so Sicilian! Fennel, oranges, and olives have grown plentifully in Sicily for generations so this fabulous combination is well embedded in authentic Sicilian cooking.

2 fennel bulbs, trimmed, quartered, and cored
6 to 8 oranges, peeled and segmented
2 cups pitted calamata olives or Sicilian green olives
1 red onion, thinly sliced
1/2 cup extra virgin olive oil
Juice of 2 lemons
Kosher salt
Pepper, freshly ground

Slice the fennel bulbs into thin crescents. Remove all the white skin from the oranges, using a sharp paring knife. Cut the oranges by running the knife between each segment, leaving the membrane behind. (You may also slice seedless oranges in rounds if that is easier for you, but still cut away rind to remove all the white skin.) Toss all the ingredients together and serve immediately.

Schiacciate (Marinated Olive Salad)

Schiacciate means "smashed" in Italian.

1 quart large Sicilian green olives, with pits
1/2 red onion, slivered
4 stalks celery, sliced
2 to 3 tablespoons fresh Italian parsley, chopped
1 teaspoon dried oregano
1/2 cup olive oil
1/4 cup red wine vinegar

Using a kitchen mallet, smash the olives so they crack. Combine all the ingredients and chill.

Sicilian Potato Salad

This is a great summer recipe-perfect for a picnic. Serve this salad at room temperature or warm. It can be made the day before and reheated quickly in a sauté pan.

3 pounds red potatoes washed, not peeled
1/2 pound green beans, blanched, snipped and left whole
1 small red onion, sliced into thin 1/2 moons
4 stalks celery, sliced into thin 1/2 moons
1 cup pitted calamata olives, roughly chopped
1/2 cup white balsamic vinegar
2 tablespoons Dijon mustard
2 tablespoons chopped Italian parsley
1 cup extra virgin olive oil
Salt
Pepper

Cut potatoes into 1/4-inch slices, cover with water in a large pot, and bring to a boil. Turn off the heat and cover for 10 minutes or until the potatoes are cooked through but still firm. Drain potatoes, do not cool. Blanch the beans in lightly salted boiling water for 7 minutes. Drain and cool. Slice the red onion and celery into thin 1/2 moon slices. Roughly chop the calamata olives. To make the dressing, place the vinegar, mustard, and parsley in a mixing bowl. Whisk in the oil to form an emulsion. Combine all the ingredients. Season with salt and pepper.

Tomato, Onion and Mint Salad

Preheat grill.

10 Roma tomatoes
1/2 cup extra virgin olive oil
Salt
Pepper
1 medium red onion, thinly sliced
1/4 cup roughly chopped fresh mint
1 teaspoon ground cumin
1/4 cup red wine vinegar

Rub the whole tomatoes with some of the olive oil and season with salt and pepper. Char the tomato skins on a hot grill. Grill or broil the onion to sweat it, enhancing it with a little char and smoky flavor. Quarter the tomatoes. Combine all the ingredients in a bowl. Serve at room temperature or chilled.

Note: This salad can be made with grape tomatoes and also without grilling the tomatoes and onion.

Traditionally, fresh tomatoes would not be served at a Saint Joseph's table because the feast day occurs in spring, and tomatoes are not ready to harvest until later in the summer. Today, we have the luxury of hot-house tomatoes, and a few varieties can be found year-round. Roma tomatoes are usually pretty good, grape tomatoes have a sweet flavor most of the year, and vine-ripened hot-house tomatoes are also good bets during the winter and spring months. To enhance the flavor of off-season tomatoes, toss them with a little extra virgin olive oil and kosher salt.

Roasted Red Pepper Salad

8 to 12 fresh red peppers
1/4 cup olive oil
1 bunch scallions, slivered
1 clove garlic, chopped
Salt
Pepper

Place the peppers on a hot grill and char on all sides. Do not rub them with oil, and do not burn them. Allow the peppers to cool and peel off the outer skin. Remove the seeds and julienne into 1/2-inch strips. Mix with the oil, scallions, garlic, salt, and pepper. Can be prepared up to a week ahead of time.

Peppers can be roasted on the grill, over an open flame, on a gas stove, over an open fire pit, or in an oven broiler. The faster they char, the firmer they will be when done. Properly charred peppers will have some black and some red skin. The peppers actually steam in their skin. This gives them a wonderful smoky flavor.

Verdure/Vegetables

Swiss Chard with Tomatoes

Stuffed Zucchini

Pickled Beets

Pickled Eggplant

Pickled Peppers

Marinated Mushrooms

Stuffed Artichokes Mama Dano

Artichoke Fritters

Beans and Greens

Green Beans and Tomatoes

Carduni Fritti (Fried Cardoons)

Cippolini Onions with Raisins

Dandelion Greens with Garlic

Fava Beans and Garlic

Breaded Eggplant Cutlets

Baked *Finocchi* (Fennel)

Rapini Greens with Raisins and Pine Nuts

Swiss Chard Patties

Roasted Wild Mushrooms

Baked Cauliflower

Verdure/Vegetables

While Sicilians would never think of sitting down to a meal without bread and pasta is a staple, vegetables provide excitement to the menu. We anticipate the coming season of rapini, asparagus, wild greens, or tomatoes and look forward to a favorite secret stash of wild mushrooms. Whether cooked simply and mixed with olive oil, salt and pepper, or deftly combined with pasta or eggs. vegetables add color to meals. We Sicilians love our fresh vegetables and enjoy lots of them with meals. A typical meal at home might include a plate of roasted peppers, pickled beets, rapini greens, some sautéed wild mushrooms, and maybe a little raw fennel with lemon and olive oil. The sky is the limit. We compete to see who has the best in-season vegetables and who can bring out the natural flavors in the simplest, purest form.

Everyone over the age of forty in my family carries a knife and a paper bag under the seat of their car just in case a patch of dandelions or erba-amari is spotted on the side of the road. My father takes me on tours to show me his secret caches of watercress and burdocks.

Swiss Chard with Tomatoes

1 pound Swiss chard, washed
1 large onion, slivered
1/4 cup olive oil
1 clove garlic

2 Roma tomatoes, chopped (or 1 14-ounce can kitchen-cut tomatoes)
Salt
Pepper

Remove chard stems from leaves and cut into 3- to 4-inch pieces. Place stems in boiling water for 3 to 4 minutes. Add the leaves and cook for 8 minutes or until tender but firm. In a separate saucepan, sauté the onion in oil. Add the garlic and tomatoes and sauté for 3 to 5 minutes. Drain water from the chard, leaving just enough to form a soupy mixture. Mix the tomatoes and chard, and season to taste with salt and pepper.

Stuffed Zucchini

Preheat oven to 350°F.

3 6- to 8-inch zucchini, cut in half lengthwise
1/2 cup finely chopped onions
1 clove garlic, minced
1 cup seasoned Italian bread crumbs
1/4 cup olive oil
1/2 cup chopped flatleaf parsley

2 tablespoons chopped fresh mint
2 eggs
Salt
Pepper
1/2 cup grated Parmigiano-Romano (or omit for Saint Joseph's table)

Scrape out the insides of the zucchinis to hollow them out like canoes. Chop up the zucchini that you removed. In a bowl, combine chopped zucchini with the rest of ingredients (except the cheese) and mix together. Season the resulting *"battuto"* to taste with salt and pepper. Stuff the zucchinis so they are heaping full. Sprinkle with cheese (if using) and place on a cookie sheet. Bake at 350°F for 20 to 30 minutes. The zucchini should be tender, and stuffing should be a little crunchy on top. Cut the stuffed zucchinis in thirds and serve as a great side dish.

Pickled Beets

Preheat oven to 350°F.

3 pounds beets, washed
Olive oil to coat
Salt
Pepper
1 quart white vinegar
2 cups brown sugar
1/2 cup diced red onion
2 teaspoons ground cloves

Choose medium-sized beets with the leaves still attached. This ensures that they are fresh. Be sure to save the leaves for a salad or cooked greens. I prefer to roast rather than boil beets. They retain more flavor, color, and vitamins when roasted.

Place the beets in a roasting pan. Rub with olive oil, salt, and pepper, and cover with foil. Roast in the oven for 30 to 45 minutes. Beets are done if tender when pierced with a fork. Peel the beets and slice or cube into uniform-sized pieces. Mix with the other ingredients.

Note: This recipe can be prepared several days ahead of time.

Pickled Eggplant

1 cup chopped onion
2 cloves garlic, chopped
2 tablespoons oregano
2 tablespoons chopped fresh parsley
1 tablespoon crushed red pepper
1/2 teaspoon salt

1/4 teaspoon pepper
2 cups olive oil
6 cups white vinegar
2 cups water
2 cups sugar
6 small, firm eggplants

Combine the onion, garlic, oregano, parsley, red pepper, salt, pepper and olive oil in a large bowl, and set aside. Bring the vinegar, water, and sugar to a boil in a 4- to 6-quart pot. Peel and cut eggplants into 1/2-inch slices and blanch for about 3 minutes. Remove the eggplant with a slotted spoon and allow to drain. Place the warm eggplant in the bowl and toss with other ingredients. Pack the seasoned eggplant in 1-quart glass jars. Pour excess oil over the top. Fill the jars the rest of the way with the vinegar-water mix. Store in the refrigerater for up to a month.

Pickled Peppers

Make these in the summer when they're plentiful and inexpensive. Find banana peppers or sweet red peppers in your local farmers market and can them. They're wonderful to have year-round! This recipe makes about 20 pints.

8 quarts peppers (20-30), seeded
10 cups cider vinegar
8 cups water
2 tablespoons Kosher salt
5 pounds sugar
1 tablespoon olive oil per jar (if canning)

Cut peppers into 1/2-inch strips. Bring the vinegar, water, salt, and sugar to a boil in a large pot and cook for 15 minutes.

Now you have two choices: Either put the peppers in canning jars for long-term storage, or refrigerate them for immediate use.

• For immediate use, add the peppers to the boiling mixture on the stove, remove from heat and allow the peppers to cool naturally. Place peppers in jars and refrigerate.

• To can for storage, pack the peppers in sterilized jars. Add one tablespoon of olive oil to each jar. Fill the jars with the hot vinegar mix up to half an inch from the rim. Seal the jars and put them in a large pot with cold water. Bring the water to a boil and process the jars for 10 minutes. After removing jars from the water, you should hear a series of pops. That is the sound of the jars sealing. Make sure the jars are clean and sealed. Store them in a cool place (in a basement or a closet) for up to a year.

Marinated Mushrooms

6 cups white vinegar
2 cups water
3 pounds small fresh mushrooms, cleaned
1 cup chopped onion
2 cloves garlic, chopped
2 tablespoons oregano

2 tablespoons chopped fresh parsley
1 tablespoon crushed red pepper
Olive oil
Salt
Pepper

Bring the vinegar and water to a boil in a 4- to 6-quart pot. Add the mushrooms and blanch for about 3 minutes. Remove the mushrooms with a slotted spoon and drain. Place mushrooms in a glass jar and add the other ingredients. Fill the jar half way with the vinegar mix and the rest of the way with olive oil. Store in the refrigerator for up to 3 months.

Marinated Mushrooms

Stuffed Artichokes Mama Dano

Artichokes:

1 lemon, juiced
Water
6 medium artichokes
Olive oil for drizzling
2 bay leaves

Stuffing _(Battuto)_:

1 cup finely chopped onions
1 clove garlic, minced
1 cup seasoned Italian bread crumbs
1/2 cup olive oil
1/2 cup grated Parmigiano or Romano
1/2 cup chopped flatleaf parsley
2 tablespoons fresh mint
Salt
Pepper

In a small bowl, combine the lemon juice with enough water to immerse an artichoke. Reserve the lemon. To prepare the artichokes, trim the tough outer leaves and cut the stalks even with the bottom of the artichokes, so they will sit level while cooking. Reserve the stalks. Cut the leaves across the top and loosen by spreading them apart with your fingers. Remove the sharp, spiny inner leaves and "hairs" by scraping the inside of the spiny bottom with a teaspoon. As you trim and clean each artichoke, immerse it in the lemon water to prevent browning. With both hands, gently loosen the leaves so the artichoke opens like the bloom of a flower.

Combine all the stuffing ingredients in a bowl. Loosely place stuffing between the individual leaves and in the artichoke cavity. Do not pack tight or the stuffing will harden when cooked.

Stand the artichokes up in a pot or pan with shallow sides in which all the artichokes will fit comfortably. Place the stalks between the artichokes, being careful not to crowd them. Fill the pot with water about a quarter of the way up the artichokes. Drizzle the artichokes tops with a little olive oil. Add the reserved lemon and bay leaves to the cooking liquid. Cook covered at a slow boil for 30 to 45 minutes or until artichokes are tender. Test for doneness by inserting a long cooking fork all the way through the 'choke to the heart. Remove artichokes from the pan with a slotted spoon and drain. Do not leave them in the cooking liquid or the stuffing will become soggy. Serve at room temperature.

When cooked properly, artichokes have grades of tenderness. The outer leaves remain tough and inedible, but the inside of the leaves will have some tasty "meat" that you can eat by scraping it between your teeth.
A little stuffing on the leaf enhances the flavor. As you get closer to the "heart" of the artichoke, the leaves gradually become tenderer, until they are totally edible. The prize is the artichoke heart, the most wonderful and flavorful part of the artichoke.

Artichoke Fritters

Fritters:
2 16-ounce cans quartered artichoke hearts (water packed), chopped
1/2 medium red onion, diced small
1 sweet red bell pepper, diced small
1 tablespoon basil, chiffonade
1 tablespoon fennel fronds, if available
Zest and juice of 1 lemon
4 extra-large eggs
1 cup flour
1 tablespoon dried oregano
1 tablespoon mint, fresh or dried
3 scallions, diced
Salt
Pepper
Cooking oil

Lemon Aioli:
2 cups mayonnaise
1 clove garlic, minced
3 teaspoons lemon zest
2 teaspoons chopped parsley
Juice of 1 lemon
1 shallot, diced
2 tablespoons Dijon mustard

To prepare the fritters, combine all the ingredients in a large bowl to form a batter. Heat about an inch of oil. Drop scoops of batter into the skillet, using a soup spoon. Fry the batter until light brown and crispy. Remove the fritters from the oil with a slotted spoon and allow them to rest on paper towels. Arrange on a platter and serve with lemon aioli.

To make the aioli, combine all the ingredients in a mixing bowl.

Beans and Greens

1/2 cup olive oil
1 medium onion, diced
2 cloves chopped garlic
1 cup white wine
1 pound (2 cups) dried navy beans, washed
 and soaked overnight
4 quarts water or chicken or vegetable stock

1 tablespoon chopped fresh rosemary
2 bunch escarole greens, washed and drained and
 chopped in 2 inch pieces (see pages 40-41)
Salt
Pepper
Extra virgin olive oil for drizzling

Heat oil in an 8-quart pot, and sauté the onion until translucent. Add the garlic and wine, and reduce. Add the beans and cover with 4 quarts of water or stock. Add the rosemary. Bring to a boil, reduce the heat, and simmer until the water is absorbed and the beans are tender, about 1 hour. If necessary, add more water. Add the escarole to the pot and simmer for 10 minutes. Season to taste with salt and pepper. Ladle into serving bowls and drizzle with extra virgin olive oil.

Green Beans and Tomato

2 pounds fresh green beans
1/2 cup olive oil
1 onion, slivered
2 cloves garlic, smashed

1 14-ounce-can tomatoes, kitchen cut
1 teaspoon dried oregano
Salt
Pepper

This is a great summer recipe! Perfect for a picnic.

Cook the green beans for 6 minutes in a large pot of boiling, salted water. Heat the oil in a separate pot and sauté the onion. Add the garlic, tomatoes, oregano, and green beans. Season with salt and pepper to taste. Serve warm, cold, or at room temperature.

Carduni Fritti/Fried Cardoons

2 pounds domestic cardoons (or wild burdocks)
Cold water
Lemon juice
1/4 cup seasoned Italian bread crumbs
4 extra-large eggs
3 tablespoons chopped fresh parsley
1 teaspoon dried oregano
1 clove garlic, chopped
4 tablespoons grated Parmesan cheese
1 teaspoon kosher salt
1/2 teaspoon black pepper
1 cup salad oil /olive oil blend

To prepare the cardoons, separate the stalks and rinse well. Discard any discolored outer stalks and leaves. Trim the base, tip, and outermost stalks, removing strings from the stalks as you would from celery. A potato peeler works well. Cut the cardoons crosswise into 5-inch lengths, then lengthwise into 1/2-inch strips. Soak the cardoons briefly in cold water with lemon juice to prevent discoloring. Bring 4 to 6 quarts of salted water to a boil. Add the cardoons and simmer for 15 minutes or until tender. Drain well and cool quickly.

To make the batter, mix all the ingredients, except the cardoons and the oil, in a mixing bowl. Heat the oil in a large skillet over medium flame until the oil bubbles when the cardoons are placed in the pan. Dip stalks in the batter two or three at a time. Fry the stalks until golden brown, regulating the heat so the oil continues to bubble gently but does not cook the cardoons too quickly. Remove the cardoons to a warming plate covered with paper towels. Season to taste with salt and pepper. Serve immediately or reheat in the oven (not in a microwave) to maintain a crispy crust.

Makes about 30 pieces per pound. If serving warm, sprinkle with extra grated Parmesan. Can also be served cold.

This recipe calls for domestic cardoons, but wild burdocks picked in early spring may be substituted and can be prepared in the same way. Wild burdocks are much tastier than the domestic version, are tenderer, and require less boiling time than do cardoons. Cardoons are not always available in supermarkets, so if you find them, consider buying extra. Clean, trim, and boil them, and freeze them in ziplock freezer bags. Be sure to drain and dry well before battering if being used for *Carduni Fritti*.

61

Cippolini Onions with Raisins

Preheat oven to 350°F.

1 pound *cippolini* onions, peeled
1/4 cup olive oil
1/2 cup balsamic vinegar
1/4 cup sugar
1/2 cup sultana raisins

Blanch the onions for 3 minutes in boiling water. Cool in an ice bath and drain. Place the onions in a baking dish with the olive oil, vinegar, sugar, and raisins. Bake covered at 350°F for 30 to 40 minutes.

Dandelion Greens with Garlic

8 to 10 quarts water
2 tablespoons salt
3 bunches dandelion greens, chopped into 2-inch pieces, washed and drained (see page 40)
1/2 cup extra virgin olive oil
3 tablespoons chopped roasted garlic
Salt
Pepper

Bring water to a rolling boil in a large pot. Add 2 tablespoons of salt. Boil the greens for 5 to 7 minutes, checking for tenderness. Strain and rinse with cold water. Toss with the oil and garlic, and season with salt and pepper to taste.

Note: Rapini greens may be substituted for dandelion greens if available.

Fava Beans and Garlic

1/2 red onion, diced
2 tablespoons olive oil
2 16-ounce cans fava beans, drained and rinsed
2 cloves garlic, chopped
10 to 15 leaves fresh basil, chiffonade
1/2 cup extra virgin olive oil
Salt
Pepper

In ancient times, fava beans were used as a form of currency. So the saying goes: "if you keep a fava in your pocket, you will never go hungry, and you will never go broke."

Sauté the onions in olive oil in a large skillet until translucent. Add the fava beans, stirring while cooking for 1 minute. Add the garlic and cook for 2 minutes on medium heat. Allow to cool. Add the basil and olive oil, and season with salt and pepper to taste. Serve at room temperature.

Breaded Eggplant Cutlets

Breaded and fried, the flavors are wonderful!

2 eggplants, peeled
2 cups flour
3 eggs, beaten
1/2 cup milk

2 cups seasoned Italian bread crumbs
Olive oil
Salt
Pepper

Slice the eggplant into 1/2-inch rounds. Set up 3 separate bowls. Put flour in one bowl, egg and milk in another, and bread crumbs in the third. Place each slice of eggplant first in the flour, then in the eggwash, then in the bread crumbs, forming a bread crumb coating on each slice of eggplant. Heat about an inch of olive oil in a large skillet until oil bubbles when the eggplant is placed in the pan. Brown the eggplant on both sides, regulating the heat so the oil continues bubbling gently but does not cook the eggplant too quickly. Remove the eggplant to a warming plate covered with paper towels. Season to taste with salt and pepper. Serve immediately or reheat in the oven (not in a microwave) to maintain a crispy crust.

Baked *Finocchi* (Fennel)

Preheat oven to broil.

4 bulbs fennel, quartered but not cored
3 quarts chicken stock
3/4 stick butter
1/4 cup grated Pecorino-Romano

1/4 cup bread crumbs *ammudicata*
  (see page 24)
Salt
Pepper

Boil the fennel in the stock for about 10 minutes. Remove the fennel from the liquid and place in a baking pan. Dot with butter and sprinkle with the cheese and bread crumbs. Season to taste with salt and pepper. Brown the fennel under the broiler.

Rapini with Raisins and Pine Nuts

The rapini greens are prepared in much the same way as dandelion greens in the Dandelion Greens Salad on page 41, and dandelion greens could be substituted for rapini greens in this recipe.

8 to 10 quarts water
2 tablespoons salt
3 bunches rapini greens, washed,
    drained, stemmed, and halved (flowers intact)
1/2 cup extra virgin olive oil
1 teaspoon balsamic vinegar

2 cloves garlic, chopped
1/2 cup honey
1/2 cup sultana raisins
1/2 cup pine nuts, toasted
Salt
Pepper

In a large sauce pot, bring salted water to a rolling boil. Add the rapini stems and cook for 3 minutes. Add the leaves and flowers and cook for 4 minutes more. Check for tenderness. Strain and rinse with cold water. Toss the greens with the olive oil, balsamic vinegar, garlic, honey, raisins, and pine nuts. Salt and pepper to taste. Serve at room temperature or hot.

Note: Can be made the day before and reheated quickly in a sauté pan.

Swiss Chard Patties

This recipe makes about 16 2-1/2-inch diameter patties to the pound.

1 pound Swiss chard, washed
8 to 10 cups water
4 eggs
3 tablespoons fresh parsley
3 tablespoons grated *Parmesan* or *Romano* (or omit for Saint Joseph's table)
1 teaspoon dried oregano
1/2 teaspoon ground black pepper
1 teaspoon kosher salt
2 tablespoons olive oil
1/4 cup seasoned Italian bread crumbs
3/4 cup vegetable-olive oil mix

To prepare the Swiss chard, separate the stems from the leaves. If stems are wider than half an inch, slice in half lengthwise. Cut the stems into 2-1/2- to 3-inch lengths. In a pot, bring water to a boil. Add stems and cook for 3 minutes. Add the leaves and continue cooking for 7 minutes. Drain the chard and stop the cooking process by placing in ice water. Drain again and squeeze out excess water by hand. Place the chard in a mixing bowl. Add the remaining ingredients, mixing well.

To cook the patties, heat half the oil in a skillet on medium-high heat. Form golf-ball-size balls and place them in the hot pan. Flatten them slightly with the back of a spatula. Sauté until well browned, turning until cooked through. Add extra oil as needed. Place patties on a plate with paper towels to absorb excess oil. Sprinkle with additional grated cheese, if using.

*Note: Escarole may be substituted
for Swiss Chard.*

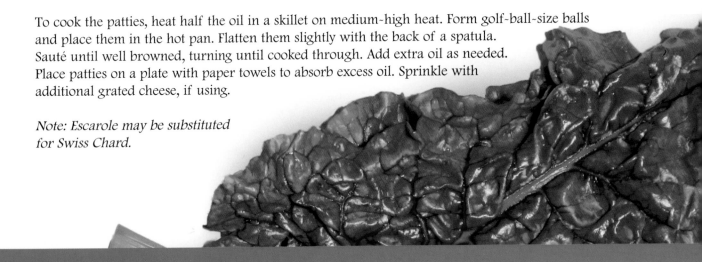

Roasted Wild Mushrooms

Preheat oven to 350°F.

8 ounces shiitake mushrooms, stemmed
16 ounces cremini mushrooms, cut in halves or thirds
2 shallots, slivered
1 tablespoon chopped fresh rosemary
1/2 cup olive oil

3 tablespoons walnut oil
2 tablespoons balsamic vinegar
2 tablespoons fresh parsley, chopped
Salt
Pepper

Tear the shiitake into large pieces. Place the shiitake and cremini in a baking dish, toss with the shallots, rosemary, and olive oil. Cover with foil and bake in the oven for 30 to 40 minutes. Remove and toss with the walnut oil, balsamic vinegar, and parsley. Season with salt and pepper.

This dish can be cooked ahead and reheated.

Baked Cauliflower

Preheat oven to 350°F.

1 head cauliflower
8 quarts water
6 tablespoons (3/4 stick) butter
1/4 cup grated Pecorino-Romano cheese

1/4 cup *ammudicata* (see page 24)
Salt
Pepper

Remove excess leaves from the cauliflower head. Bring salted water to a boil in a pot large enough to hold the whole head. Place the cauliflower in the pot. Boil for 5 minutes, turn off the burner, cover the pot, and let it rest for 10 minutes. Remove the cauliflower from the pot, cool under running water, and separate into florets. Place the florets in a casserole dish, dot with butter, sprinkle with cheese and *ammudicata*. Bake for 15-20 minutes, until the cheese and bread crumbs brown a bit and the cauliflower is hot.

Minestre/Soups

Lentil Soup

Minestrone

Pasta Fagioli

Zuppa di Pesce

Swiss Chard Soup

Maccu di Favi (Fava Bean Soup)

Maccu di San Giuseppe

Minestre/Soups

Lentil soup is the traditional Saint Joseph's day soup. In Sicilian culture, lentils represent humility and symbolize good luck. I have included a few other soups that my family enjoys and that might fit into your feast day menu. Soups are a wonderfully inexpensive way to make a meal in any culture, particularly when you need to stretch ingredients. Some of my most memorable childhood meals consisted of a simple vegetable minestra with homemade bread and a salad.

Lentil Soup

The traditional Saint Joseph's day soup.

2 stalks celery, diced
2 carrots diced
1 medium onion, diced
1/2 cup olive oil
1 clove chopped garlic
1 14-ounce can kitchen-cut tomatoes
1 teaspoon fresh thyme
1 teaspoon dried oregano

2 tablespoons chopped parsley
1/2 teaspoon black pepper
1 gallon water
4 vegetable boullion cubes
3 bay leaves
1 pound lentils, rinsed
1 teaspoon kosher salt

Sauté the celery, carrots, and onion in oil in a large pot until translucent. Add the garlic, water, tomatoes, and boullion cubes. Bring the mixture to a boil and add the herbs and lentils. Boil for 5 minutes. Reduce the heat and simmer for 30 to 40 minutes until the lentils are tender. Season to taste with salt and pepper. Finish with 2 to 3 tablespoons of olive oil.

Minestrone Soup

Minestrone is an Italian soup of pasta, beans, and seasonal vegetables. Its literal translation is the "Big Soup," meaning it has lots of ingredients. This recipe is open to many different interpretations. The one below is my family's common, everyday recipe.

1 cup diced onions
1 cup diced celery
1 cup diced carrots
1 cup diced potatoes
1/2 cup olive oil
1 tablespoon chopped garlic
2 cups diced zucchini
1 cup canned Roma tomatoes with juices, chopped
1 gallon water
4 vegetable bouillon cubes
2 bay leaves
1 tablespoon dried oregano
1 cup fresh green beans
2 cups cooked cannellini beans or chickpeas
2 cups chopped escarole greens
Crust of *Parmigiano-Reggiano*
2 cups cooked *ditalini* pasta

Sauté the onions, celery, carrots, and potatoes in the oil in a large stock pot until the onions are translucent. Add the garlic and cook 2 minutes. Add the zucchini and cook 3 minutes. Add the tomatoes, water, bouillon, and spices and bring to a boil. Add the green beans and cannellini or chickpeas and cook 15 minutes. Add the escarole and the crust from the cheese. When ready to serve, add cooked ditalini pasta.

Pasta Fagioli

Serves 12 to 14

A traditional soup consisting of pasta and assorted beans, pasta fagioli is a good choice for your Saint Joseph's day buffet if you are trying for simplicity and ease. It is inexpensive a-meal-in-itself and can take the place of the soup and pasta courses if you like. It can also be prepared two to three days ahead. To avoid soggy, overcooked pasta, do not combine the pasta with the beans until ready to serve.

1 pound ditalini pasta, cooked, drained,
 and cooled
1/2 cup olive oil
1 small onion, diced
6 stalks celery, diced
2 cloves garlic, crushed
2 15.5-ounce cans cannelini beans
2 15.5-ounce cans red kidney beans
2 15.5-ounce cans chickpeas
2 tablespoons dried oregano

2 tablespoons dried basil
1 bunch fresh parsley, chopped
Salt
Pepper
1 quart water
1 28-ounce can diced tomatoes or 4 fresh
 tomatoes, diced
Grated Romano cheese (optional)

Drizzle the cooked pasta with 2 tablespoons of the olive oil, and set aside, or refrigerate if preparing ahead. Sauté the onions and celery in the remaining oil in a large pot until the onion is translucent. Add the garlic and sauté for 2 minutes. Drain and rinse the beans and and add chickpeas to the pot. Season with oregano, basil, parsley, salt, and pepper. Add the water and tomatoes. Bring to a boil and simmer for 20 to 30 minutes, stirring often so the beans don't stick. If it is not Saint Joseph's day, add the cheese for more flavor.

If prepping ahead, stop here. Cool and refrigerate. When ready to serve, reheat bean soup mix. When hot, add the pasta and stir until hot. Serve in a nice ceramic soup urn, crock pot, or chafing dish, or simply from the pot on the stove.

Zuppa di Pesce (Fish Soup)

Fish soup is precisely what it sounds like. Vary the recipe as much as you like. Include tomatoes or not, potatoes or not. The soup will gain flavor with each seafood addition. You are making your own broth in the pot, so there is no need for fish stock or clam juice. A good broth and fresh fish is all you need.

1/2 cup olive oil
1 onion, slivered
4 tender inner stalks celery, cut thin on bias
Celery leaves from stalks
1/2 bulb fennel, trimmed, cored, and thinly sliced
1 pound shrimp
2 cups white wine
1 14-ounce can diced tomatoes
2 quarts water
1 pound cod, cut in 2-inch pieces
12 clams
2 pounds mussels
1/4 cup fresh parsley
1/4 cup fresh oregano or 1 tablespoon dried oregano
Salt
Pepper

In a large braiser or stock pot, heat the olive oil over medium heat. Sauté the onions, celery, and fennel until the onions are translucent. Add the shrimp and sauté briefly until they turn orange and release a little flavor into the pot. Remove the shrimp and reserve. Add the wine to deglaze, and reduce by half. Add the tomatoes and water, and bring to a boil. You may stop at this point. When you are almost ready to serve, add the clams. When they begin to open, add the mussels, shrimp, and herbs. Season with salt and pepper to taste. Add the cod just before serving. It will cook very quickly. Serve the stew over a nice hunk of bread.

Swiss Chard Soup

1/2 cup olive oil
1 medium onion, diced
4 ribs celery, diced
1 medium carrot, diced
2 bunches Swiss chard, diced bite-size and washed

8 quarts water
4 vegetable bouillon cubes
2 Roma tomatoes, diced
Extra virgin olive oil for drizzling

In a large stock pot, heat the oil over medium heat. Add the onions, celery, and carrot, and cook for 3 minutes. Add the Swiss chard, cover, and steam for 10 minutes. Add the water, bouillon and tomatoes. Bring to a boil, lower the heat, and simmer for 15 minutes. Ladle into bowls and drizzle with extra virgin olive oil.

Maccu di Favi (Fava Bean Soup)

1 pound dried fava beans, rinsed
2 quarts water, salted
1/2 cup extra virgin olive oil
1 onion, diced
1/2 medium bulb fennel, diced

1 teaspoon fennel seed, roasted in oven until
  aromatic and ground to powder
Sicilian sea salt
Crushed red pepper
Fronds of 1 fennel bulb, diced

Add the fava beans to two quarts of hot salted water in an 8-quart pot and bring to a boil. Cover the pot, turn off the heat, and let rest for 10 minutes. Drain the beans, reserving the liquid for broth. Peel the favas. In a dry 8-quart pot, heat most of the olive oil (reserving some for drizzling), add the onions and fennel (bulb dice only), and sauté until the onions are translucent. Add the reserved broth and fennel powder. Bring to a boil and cook for about 40 minutes or until beans are cooked through. Purée the soup with a burr mixer or in a blender. Season with salt, red pepper, and fennel fronds. Ladle into bowls and drizzle with extra virgin olive oil.

This recipe can be made a day or two ahead and reheated when ready to serve.

Maccu di San Giuseppe

This mixed bean soup is a Saint Joseph's day staple for many families. Make it a day or two before your feast; soups are always better the second day.

1/2 cup olive oil
1 medium onion, diced
4 stalks celery, diced
1 tablespoon fennel seeds
1/4 cup fennel fronds, chopped
1 12-ounce can diced tomatoes
8 quarts water
1 cup dried lentils
1 15.5-ounce can butter beans, drained and rinsed
1 15.5-ounce can chickpeas, drained and rinsed
1 15.5-ounce can cannellini beans, drained and rinsed
1 15.5-ounce can kidney beans, drained and rinsed
4 vegetable bouillon cubes
4 cups any greens, washed and chopped (spinach, chard, escarole, borage)
Salt
Crushed red pepper
Extra virgin olive oil for drizzling

Heat the oil in a large stock pot over medium heat. Add the onions and celery and sauté until onions are translucent. Add the fennel seeds, fronds, and diced tomatoes. Add the water and lentils and bring to a boil. Add the beans and bouillon, and simmer for 1 hour or until lentils are well cooked. Add the greens and cook until wilted. Season to taste with salt and red pepper. Ladle into bowls and drizzle with extra virgin olive oil.

Pasta e Grani/
Pasta and Grains

Pasta con Sarde

Pasta Pomodoro with Eggplant and *Ricotta*

Couscous with Raisins and Pine Nuts

Farro, Fava and Feta

Ditalini with Lentils

Pasta and Broccoli

Pasta with Cauliflower

Mushroom and Barley *Risotto*

Rosemary *Polenta*

Pasta e Grani/Pasta and Grains

When hosting a Saint Joseph's table, I highly recommend making the pasta con sarde. This is the traditional Saint Joseph's day pasta. Classically Sicilian, it is made with wild fennel, sardines, fresh tomato sauce, sultana raisins, and toasted pine nuts. Some people love it, while others absolutely cannot abide the sardines. So why not make some of the dish without sardines? The other pasta dishes in this section are some wonderful family recipes that can be made anytime or in addition to the pasta con sarde on your buffet. After all, what kind of Sicilian cookbook would this be with only one pasta recipe?

Sicilian cooking is a mirror of its history. Each conquerer contributed to the Sicilian table. The Romans brought wheat and grains, such as farro and barley. The Arabs brought couscous, rice, citrus trees, and eggplant. To all of them, our thanks!

Pasta con Sarde

1 small onion, diced
1 fennel bulb with fronds, diced
Olive oil
2 tablespoons capers
1 cup sultana raisins
2 pounds perciatelli pasta
3 quarts homemade *Pomodoro* (see page 80)
1/2 cup toasted pine nuts
1 can sardines
Parsley for garnish

Sauté the onions and fennel in the oil until translucent.
Add the capers and the raisins. Continue to sauté for 3
minutes, and reserve. Remove sardines from water, chop
roughly, and reserve.Cook the pasta according to package
directions and heat the marinara sauce, which should be
on thin side. Spread a little sauce on a serving platter. Heap
the pasta onto the platter, cover with sauce, and top with
the fennel, raisins, nuts, and sardines. Stir slightly. Garnish
with breadcrumbs. Serve hot. Try not to put this dish in the
oven, as it dries out easily.

Perciatelli is the traditional
Saint Joseph's day pasta. I
have always used penne pasta
with this dish because it holds
up well. But, as usual, my
father put in his two cents,
saying, "My mother always
used perciatelli." Well, I
found some of this unusual
pasta and picked up a few
pounds. I used it during a
cooking class I teach about
Saint Joseph's day, and it came
out really well! Now we serve
this long, hollow spaghetti-
like pasta at every Saint
Joseph's day celebration.
Perciatelli is thick enough to
hold up well to the sauce and
the time it spends on the
buffet, and it's so unique that
everyone asks about it. Try it!

Pasta Pomodoro
with Eggplant and Ricotta

Preheat oven to 350°F.

Pomodoro sauce
1 onion, diced
Olive oil for sautéing
2 cloves garlic, crushed
3 24-ounce cans kitchen-cut tomatoes
2 tablespoons dried basil
2 tablespoons dried oregano
Salt
Pepper

Roasted eggplant
1 or 2 eggplants, peeled and cubed
2 cloves garlic, crushed
1/4 cup olive oil
Salt
Pepper

Herbed ricotta
1 cup ricotta
1/2 cup mozzarella, shredded
1/4 cup grated Romano or Parmesan
1/4 cup fresh basil chiffonade or 1 tablespoon dried basil
1/4 cup chopped fresh mint or 1 tablespoon dried mint
1/4 cup chopped fresh parsley or 1 tablespoon dried parsley

To make the sauce, sauté the onions in the oil in a large pot until translucent. Add the garlic, tomatoes, and herbs. Slowly bring the sauce to a boil and simmer gently for 20 minutes.

To cook the eggplant, place cubes in a baking dish. Add garlic and olive oil, and sprinkle with salt and pepper to taste. Cover the dish with foil and bake for 20 minutes or until the eggplant is soft but retains its shape.

To make the herbed ricotta, blend all the ingredients together.

Cook the pasta according to package directions and place in an oven-proof bowl or baking dish. Top with the hot pomodoro sauce, scatter the eggplant, and put the ricotta on top in small dollops. Bake for 10 minutes at 350°F. Serve with a green salad.

Couscous with Raisins and Pine Nuts

The combination of toasted pine nuts, honey, herbs, and dried fruits give this dish a distinctive Sicilian flavor with Arabian notes that stem from the Arab presence in Sicily during the island's history, one of the many cultures that have wandered through and battled to gain the lands of Sicily. This is why Sicilian cooking varies so much from Italian cooking. This dish can be prepared a day ahead and served cold.

1 16-ounce box couscous
1/2 cup dried cherries
1/2 cup dried currants
1/2 cup golden raisins
1/2 cup pine nuts, toasted
1/2 bulb fennel, diced
1/2 red onion, diced
1/2 cup honey
1/2 cup olive oil
1/4 cup red vinegar
1/4 cup chopped fresh mint
1/4 cup chopped Italian parsley
Salt
Pepper

Do not follow the directions on the box of couscous. Instead, boil 2 cups of water in a small saucepan. Place the dry couscous in a large metal mixing bowl and add the boiling water. Cover the bowl with plastic wrap to retain the steam. Once the water has been absorbed (about 10 minutes), uncover and fluff with a fork until the grains are separate and fluffy. Refrigerate to cool. Combine with all other ingredients. Serve cold or at room temperature.

Farro, Fava and Feta

Preheat oven to 350°F.

Farro is an ancient grain dating back to early Roman civilization. It resembles barley and behaves like risotto in some applications. In this recipe, simply boil and simmer the farro.

2 cups farro
8 cups water
1 cup olive oil
1-1/2 tablespoons salt
2 pounds fresh fava beans
1 cup feta cheese
1 cup walnuts, toasted
1 cup fresh basil, chiffonade
1/2 cup fresh lemon juice

Cook the farro in a 6-quart sauce pot in 6 cups of the water, a drizzle of the olive oil, and 1 tablespoon of the salt. Bring to a boil and simmer the farro until the water is absorbed. Remove the beans from their pods. Bring remaining water to a boil in a second pot, salt the water, and cook the favas for 5 minutes. Cool and slip off the favas' second skin. Shred the feta cheese. Toast the walnuts for 10 minutes at 350°F. Combine all the ingredients. Serve at room temperature.

Ditalini with Lentils

Since lentils are thought to bring good luck, this also makes a good New Year's Day meal.

2 cups lentils, rinsed
1 onion, diced
2 cloves garlic
2 vegetable bouillon cubes
1/2 + 1/4 cup olive oil
Salt 1 teaspoon + 1 teaspoon
Pepper
1 16-ounce box *ditalini* pasta
2 tablespoons chopped Italian parsley

Put the lentils into a pot with 2 quarts of water, add the onion, garlic, bouillon, 1/4 cup of olive oil, 1 teaspoon salt, and pepper to taste, bring to a boil, and simmer for 30-40 minutes until the lentils are tender and the water is absorbed. Bring 6 quarts of water to a rolling boil, add 1 teaspoon salt, add the pasta and cook for 8-10 minutes, stirring occasionally, drain pasta, and reserve 2 cups of pasta water. Toss the hot pasta with the hot lentils and 1/2 cup olive oil, adjust the thickness of sauce to desired consistency using the reserved pasta water. Garnish with parsley.

Pasta and Broccoli

1 medium potato, diced
1/2 cup extra virgin olive oil
1 medium onion, diced
3 Roma tomato, diced
1 clove garlic

2 tablespoons Italian parsley, chopped
4 cups broccoli florets and peeled sliced stems
1 16-ounce box ditalini pasta
2 vegetable bouillon cubes

Sauté the potato in 2 tablespoons of the olive oil on medium high heat for 3-4 minutes until cooked through and golden. Add the onion and sauté until translucent, add garlic to release flavor, add diced tomato and reduce heat to simmer for 4-5 minutes, set aside. Add parsley.

In a soup pot, boil 6 quarts of water (pasta will take 8 minutes to cook; broccoli will take 6 minutes to cook.) Salt your water with 1/2 tablespoon of salt. Add bouillon cubes. Add pasta and stir, wait 3 minutes and add broccoli, continue cooking for 6 minutes. Test for doneness, remove from heat and add potato-tomato mix. Stir. Add 1/4 cup of extra virgin olive oil, salt and pepper to taste.
If it is not Saint Joseph's day add some parmesan cheese to finish it off.

Pasta with Cauliflower

1 head cauliflower
1 pound small pasta shells
1 stick butter
1/4 cup fresh sage, chiffonade

Salt
Crushed red pepper
Ammudicata (see page 24).

Trim excess leaves from cauliflower head. Bring a pot of salted water to boil and add the whole head of cauliflower. Boil for 5 minutes, reduce the heat, and simmer for 10 more minutes. Remove the cauliflower from the pot. In the same water, cook the pasta according to directions on the box. Break the cauliflower into small pieces. Drain the pasta, reserving some liquid, and toss with cauliflower, butter, and sage in a large bowl. Season with salt and pepper. Add a little cooking liquid to finish the sauce. Garnish with bread crumbs.

Mushroom and Barley Risotto

3 shallots, slivered
1 12-ounce package cremini mushrooms
1 12-ounce package shiitake mushrooms
1 ounce dried porcini mushrooms
1 bunch fresh flatleaf parsley, chopped
1 tablespoon chopped fresh thyme

2 pounds barley, rinsed
1/2 cup olive oil
Water-4 quarts to start, add more as needed
4 vegetable bouillon cubes

Slice the mushrooms and grind the porcinis to powder using a handheld coffee grinder. Heat the oil in a large, heavy-bottomed pot. Add the shallots and cook for 2 minutes. Add the sliced mushrooms and cook well. Add the water, porcini powder, thyme, and bouillon. Stir frequently until the barley is cooked through and a creamy consistency is achieved, adding water as needed. Stirring frequently with a wooden spoon will give this a creamy consistency, breaking down the barley grains like risotto. Cook for 30 to 40 minutes. May be cooked the day before and reheated.

Rosemary *Polenta*

9 cups milk
1/2 cup butter (1 stick), melted
1/4 cup sugar
2 teaspoons salt
3 cups cornmeal

1 tablespoon fresh chopped rosemary
1 cup *Parmesan* (optional)
Salt
Pepper

In heavy saucepot, combine the milk, butter, sugar, and salt. Heat until steaming, but do not boil. Begin adding cornmeal in a slow, steady stream, whisking constantly. When the polenta begins to thicken, add the rosemary and *Parmesan*, and season with salt and pepper to taste. Continue stirring with a wooden spoon until the spoon stands on its own and the *polenta* starts to come away from the sides of the pot, about 10 minutes. Adjust seasonings. Pour onto a large wooden board. Let it set for 10 minutes. Cut into serving pieces and serve.

Frutti di Mare/Seafood

Roasted Cod with Pistachio-Herb Crust

Baked Cod with Lemon and Tomatoes

Marinated *Calamari* Salad

Fried *Calamari*

Arborio-Fennel Crusted *Calamari*

Stuffed Squid with Tomatoes

Mussels *Pomodoro*

Mussels *Finocchi*

Mussels *Marinara*

Mussels *Verde*

Marinated Mussel Salad

Sautéed *Calamari* with Banana Peppers

Shrimp *Pomodoro*

Scampi

Stewed Octopus

Pesce alla Messina

Swordfish with Pistachio-Orange *Tapenade*

Fried Smelt

Frutti di Mare/Seafood

Sicilians believe that fish and bread are God's gift to his people. Cod and baccalá are both commonly served on the Saint Joseph's day table, as are shrimp, mussels, calamari, and smelt. Swordfish and tuna are also indigenous to the waters around Sicily. Not all Saint Joseph's day feasts include fish, however. Although the island of Sicily is bordered by three seas and there are many fishing villages, inland communities did not have access to seafood. But since the feast occurs during Lent, there is usually seafood on the menu.

When planning, assume just a small amount of fish per person due to the extensive menu: 3- to 4-ounce portions or four portions per pound of seafood should suffice. Buy the freshest seafood available from a local fish market. Purchase your fish the day before or the day of your event! You can call ahead and preorder to ensure availability.

Roasted Cod with Pistachio-Herb Crust

Preheat oven to 375°F.

Pistachio-herb crust
1/2 cup pistachios, ground in a food processor
1/2 cup Ammundicata (see page 24)
1/2 cup fresh parsley, chopped
1/2 cup fresh mint, chopped

Cod
8 to 10 pounds cod
1 cup white wine
1/2 cup olive oil

To prepare the crust, add the bread crumbs, parsley, and mint to the ground pistachios in the food processor and pulse to mix. Place the fish in a single layer on a large sheet pan and drizzle with the oil and wine. Sprinkle each piece with one tablespoon of the pistachio-herb crust and season with salt and pepper. Bake at 375°F for 10 to 15 minutes, until the fish is white all the way through, not translucent, and the crust is golden.

Baked Cod with Lemon and Tomatoes

Preheat oven to 375°F.

8 to 10 pounds cod
10 Roma tomatoes, thinly sliced
Olive oil
Fresh lemon juice of 3-5 lemons
1 bunch-flat leaf parsley

Salt
Pepper
Ammundicata (see page 24)
Parmesan Cheese

Place the fish in a single layer on a large sheet pan, cover with the tomatoes, and drizzle with the oil and juice. Sprinkle with parsley, salt, pepper, bread crumbs, and Parmesan. Bake for 10 to 15 minutes at 375°F, until the fish is white all the way through, not translucent.

Marinated *Calamari* Salad

It may be an old wives' tale, but even famed chef Mario Batali says that boiling a wine cork in the water with the *calamari* makes the squid tenderer. Do not overcook the *calamari*, or it will be rubbery.

2 gallons water
2 lemon wedges
2 bay leaves
5 peppercorns
1 tablespoon kosher salt
1 wine cork
3 pounds fresh squid, cleaned
1 bunch parsley, chopped
4 Roma tomatoes, diced
1/2 red onion, diced
2 celery-heart stalks with leaves, slivered
1/2 cup extra virgin olive oil
1/4 cup fresh lemon juice
1/2 teaspoon crushed red pepper

Depending where you purchase the squid, it will be cleaned to differing degrees. First clean squid under cold, running water. Remove the plastic spine if there is one inside the tube. If there is grayish skin, remove it too. If the heads remain, they must be removed as well.

Bring the water to a boil in a large pot. Add the lemon wedges, bay leaves, peppercorns, salt, wine and cork. Clean squid, cut bodies cut into 1/4-inch rings and blanch for about two minutes. Drain, remove cork, and put in an ice bath to cool quickly. Combine the cooked calamari with all the remaining ingredients and refrigerate until ready to serve. This recipe can be made a day ahead.

Fried Calamari

2 pounds fresh squid
2 cups flour
3/4 cup cornmeal
2 tablespoons cornstarch
1/2 teaspoon cayenne pepper

1 tablespoon chili powder
Salt
Pepper
Olive oil for frying

Clean the squid and slice bodies into 1/4-inch rings. If the tentacles are very large, cut in half; if not, leave intact. Combine the flour, cornstarch, and seasonings, and mix well. Have a mesh strainer handy. Heat 3 inches of a good quality olive oil in a pot or pan to 350°F. When the oil is hot, drop some squid in the flour and toss to coat well, then shake off excess flour using the strainer. Fry the squid in small batches for 3 to 4 minutes until crispy and golden, being careful not to overcrowd the pan to avoid cooling down the oil. Remove the squid with a slotted spoon and drain on paper towels.

Arborio~Fennel Crusted Calamari

Preheat oven to 350°F.

2 tablespoons fennel seed, toasted
3/4 cup uncooked arborio rice
2 pounds fresh squid2 cups flour
1/2 teaspoon cayenne pepper

Salt
Pepper
Olive oil for frying

To prepare the crust, toast the fennel seeds at 350°F for 5 to 7 minutes. Grind the rice and seeds in a coffee grinder to a fine powder. Clean the squid and slice bodies into 1/4-inch rings. If the tentacles are very large, cut in half; if not, leave intact. Combine the flour, fennel seeds, Arborio rice powder and seasonings, and mix well. Have a mesh strainer handy. Heat 3 inches of a good quality olive oil in a pot or pan to 350°F. When the oil is hot, drop some squid in the flour mix and toss to coat well, shaking off excess flour using the strainer. Fry the squid in small batches in the hot oil for 3 to 4 minutes until crispy, being careful not to overcrowd to avoid cooling down the oil. Remove the squid with a slotted spoon and drain on paper towels.

Stuffed Squid with Tomatoes

Preheat oven to 350°F.

2 pounds squid
1/2 onion, minced
1/4 cup fresh parsley, chopped
1/4 cup fresh mint, chopped
2 cups fresh bread crumbs
1/2 cup grated *Parmesan*
1/4 cup + 4 tablespoons olive oil
6 Roma tomatoes, skinned, seeded, and diced
1/2 cup white wine

Clean the squid, removing plastic spines, and separate tentacles. Chop half a cup of tentacles for the stuffing, reserving the remaining tentacles for another use. Sauté the onion in 2 tablespoons of olive oil in a medium sauté pan until translucent. Add the 1/2 cup of tentacles, parsley, and mint, and sauté quickly. Remove from the heat. In a mixing bowl, combine the bread crumbs, *Parmesan*, 1/4 cup of olive oil, and the sautéed mixture. Stuff the squid using a spoon, a pastry bag, or your hands. Do not fill the entire sac and seal the ends of the sacs with toothpicks. Place the squid in a baking dish, cover with 2 tablespoons of olive oil, tomatoes, and wine. Cook in the oven at 350°F until the squid is white and stuffing is hot, 10-15 minutes. Remove toothpicks and serve immediately.

Mussels *Pomodoro*

1/2 cup olive oil
2 to 3 pounds mussels, cleaned 2 cloves garlic, chopped
5 to 6 Roma tomatoes, chopped
1/2 cup white wine
1/4 cup chopped parsley
1/2 cup fresh basil, chiffonade
Salt
Pepper

Heat the oil in a sauté pan large enough to hold all the mussels. Add the mussels, garlic, and tomatoes, and sauté 1 to 2 minutes. Add the wine, herbs, salt, and pepper. Cover to steam for 4 to 5 minutes. When mussels are open and plump, place mixture in a bowl and serve.

Clean mussels well in cold water. Remove the beards with your fingers and discard any cracked or open mussels and any that do not open after steaming. I prefer to sauté vegetables in olive oil or butter, adding the mussels to the hot oil so they sizzle, then add liquid and seasonings. This gives the mussels a burst of steam, and the heat helps them to open quickly and plump up. Cover them to steam quickly. Mussels are done in just a couple of minutes, when open.

Mussels *Finocchio*

1/2 cup heavy cream
1/2 cup sour cream
1/2 cup olive oil
3 leeks, cleaned and sliced in half moons
1 bulb fennel, cleaned, trimmed, and sliced thin

2 to 3 pounds mussels, cleaned (page 94)
1 tablespoon fresh thyme
1/2 cup Pernod
Salt
Pepper

Combine both creams in a metal bowl and whip with a wire whisk to make crème fraiche. Heat the oil in a sauté pan large enough to hold all the mussels. Add the leeks and fennel, and sauté until the fennel is tender. Add the mussels and toss to coat with oil. Add the thyme, Pernod, and season with salt and pepper to taste. Toss and cover to steam. In 4 to 5 minutes, when mussels are open and plump, add the crème fraiche, stir, and place in a serving bowl.

Mussels *Marinara*

8 gallons water
1 pound linguini
1 tablespoon salt
1/2 cup olive oil
1/2 white onion, slivered

2 cloves garlic, chopped
1 cup white wine
3 pounds mussels, cleaned (see page 94)
2 cups marinara sauce
2 tablespoons chopped Italian parsley

Bring the water to a boil. Add the salt. Cook the pasta for about 8 minutes, stirring frequently. Test for doneness. Strain and place in a serving bowl. While the pasta is cooking prepare the mussels. Heat the oil in a large shallow pot and sauté the onions until translucent. Add the garlic, wine, mussels, marinara, and parsley. Cover and steam. Mussels are done when the shell is open. Discard any mussels that do not open. Spoon the mussels and sauce over the pasta and serve.

Mussels *Verde*

Use any greens: kale, dandelions, escarole, spinach, mustard greens. Spinach and escarole can be added directly to the pan; the others should be blanched first.

4 to 6 small red potatoes
1/2 to 1 pound greens, washed and trimmed
1/2 cup olive oil
2 cloves chopped garlic
2 tablespoons chopped fresh rosemary
2 to 3 pounds mussels, cleaned (page 94)
1/2 cup white wine
Salt
Pepper

Boil the potatoes until fork tender, cool, and slice. Cut the greens into 2-inch pieces and blanch if necessary. Heat the oil in a sauté pan large enough to hold all the mussels. Add the potatoes, greens, garlic, and rosemary. Cover and cook until the garlic and rosemary have released their flavor and the potatoes and greens are hot. Add the mussels and cook for 1 minute. Add the wine and herbs, and season with salt and pepper to taste. Cover and steam for 4 or 5 minutes. When the mussels are open and plump, place them in bowl and serve.

Marinated Mussel Salad

Broth

2 cloves garlic, chopped
1/2 lemon, sliced
4 bay leaves
4 sprigs fresh thyme
4 sprigs fresh parsley
1/2 cup white wine
1 cup water
2 tablespoons olive oil
Salt
Pepper

Salad

4 green onions, sliced
4 stalks celery, thinly sliced
1/2 cup chopped parsley
1/2 cup lemon juice
1/2 cup extra virgin olive oil
2 Roma tomatoes, diced
2 to 3 pounds mussels, cleaned (see page 94)

To make the broth, in a pan large enough to hold all the ingredients, sauté the garlic in the oil to release its flavor. Add all the ingredients except the mussels. Bring the broth to a boil. Add the mussels. Cover to steam for 4 to 5 minutes. When the mussels are open and plump, place them in a mixing bowl and cool. Toss the mussels and all the ingredients together in the bowl. Chill and serve.

Sautéed *Calamari* with Banana Peppers

3 pounds *calamari* (see page 90)
4 to 6 banana peppers, halved and seeded
1 leek, cleaned
1/2 cup olive oil
Juice and zest of 2 lemons
1/2 cup fresh basil, chiffonade
Salt
Pepper

Slice the squid bodies into 1/4-inch rings. If the tentacles are very large, cut in half; if not, leave intact. Slice the peppers and the leek into thin half-moon rings. Heat the oil in a large skillet. Sauté the peppers and leeks in the hot oil for about 3 minutes. Add the calamari and toss to coat with oil. Cook quickly on high heat. Add the zest, juice, and fresh basil. Season to taste with salt and pepper. *Calamari* is done when white all the way through. Do not overcook.

Shrimp *Pomodoro*

1/4 cup olive oil
1 medium Spanish onion, sliced
4 cloves fresh garlic, chopped
4 pounds U16-20 raw shrimp
2 cups white wine

2 28-ounce cans kitchen-cut Roma tomatoes,
 with juices
1 tablespoon dried oregano
1/2 cup fresh basil, chiffonade
Salt
Pepper

Heat the oil in a large sauté pan or Dutch oven. Sauté the onion until translucent. Add the garlic and shrimp. Peel and devein shrimp. Shake the pan and turn the shrimp often to prevent the garlic from burning. Add the wine and reduce by half. Add the tomatoes and oregano. Bring to a boil and cook until the shrimp is white throughout (not translucent). Season with the basil and salt and pepper to taste. Remove from the heat and serve hot or at room temperature. Serve over pasta if you wish.

Scampi

This is a party-sized batch of shrimp! And it's a quick recipe—shrimp cook quickly.

1 tablespoon cornstarch
2 cups vegetable stock
1/2 cup olive oil
4 pounds raw U16-20 shrimp, peeled and deveined
6 large cloves garlic, chopped
2 cups white wine
1 cup Roma tomatoes, diced
1 cup chopped fresh parsley
Salt
Pepper

Dissolve the cornstarch in some of the cold vegetable stock. This will thicken your finished sauce a bit so it clings to the shrimp. Heat the oil in a large sauté pan or Dutch oven. Peel and devein shrimp. Add the shrimp and the garlic. Shake the pan and turn the shrimp often to prevent the garlic from burning. Add the wine and reduce the liquid by half. Add the tomatoes, parsley, and the rest of the stock. Bring to a boil and cook until the shrimp is white throughout (not translucent) and the stock has thickened slightly. Season with salt and pepper to taste. Remove from the heat and serve hot or at room temperature. Can be served over pasta.

Buying shrimp: Since most of the shrimp farmed in the U.S. today is frozen immediately, it is okay to buy frozen shrimp and defrost it. In fact, unless you are in a shrimp-farming region, most of the shrimp in fish-market and grocery-store display cases was previously frozen. Shrimp is labeled by size and sold cooked, raw, peeled, or shell on. If the label indicates "U16-20," there are 16 to 20 shrimp per pound. The smaller the number per pound, the larger the shrimp. If I am using 16-20 or larger, I prefer to buy raw, shell-on shrimp. For smaller sizes, I prefer peeled, raw shrimp. I almost always prefer to cook my own.

Stewed Octopus

5 pounds octopus
4 tablespoons olive oil
1 medium onion, sliced
4 cloves garlic, finely sliced
2 cups white wine
1 28-ounce can whole Roma tomatoes with juices, chopped
1 tablespoon crushed red pepper
Salt
Pepper
2 tablespoons honey
4 tablespoons capers
1 cup chopped parsley

Bring a large pot of salted water to a boil. Add the octopus and bring the water to boiling again. Cook for 3 to 4 minutes. Remove the octopus from the pot and cool under running water. Cut the octopus into 1-1/2-inch pieces. Heat the oil in a large sauté pan and add the octopus. Cook for 4 to 5 minutes. Add the onions and sauté until translucent. Add the garlic and sauté 2 to 3 more minutes. Add the wine and bring to boil over high heat. Reduce the heat and continue cooking for 4 to 5 minutes. Add the tomatoes, red pepper, salt, pepper, and honey. Cover the pan and simmer for 30 minutes. Add the capers and half of the parsley. If the octopus is still chewy, cover the pan and simmer for an additional 20 to 30 minutes. Add the remaining parsley. Serve hot or at room temperature.

Pesce alla Messina

Preheat oven to 350°F.

2 pounds swordfish or cod steaks
Salt
Pepper
1 pound all-purpose potatoes, peeled
1/3 cup extra virgin olive oil
1 medium onion, coarsely chopped
2 cloves garlic, peeled and crushed
2/3 cup dry white wine
3 cups Roma tomatoes, peeled and chopped, or
    canned kitchen-cut tomatoes
1-1/2 cups ripe green Sicilian olives,
    pitted and halved
Capers

Cut the fish into serving pieces. Season lightly
with salt and pepper and reserve. In a large
saucepan, boil the potatoes for about 10 minutes,
until a fork can be inserted but there is still some
resistance. Drain and cut into 1/4-inch slices.
Reserve. Heat the oil over medium heat in a
medium casserole. Sauté the onion and garlic for
about 5 minutes, until softened. Add the fish and
sauté, turning once, for 5 to 7 minutes or until
lightly browned. Add the wine, distribute the
tomatoes evenly in the casserole, and season with
salt and pepper. Add the potatoes, olives, and
capers. Bake until the potatoes are tender,
about 20 minutes. Serve immediately.

Chef Giardano at work in the kitchen

Swordfish with Pistachio-Orange *Tapenade*

Preheat oven to 400°F.

Prepare this recipe ahead. Cook as one of the last items to be ready.

Fish:
3 ounces swordfish per person
1/2 cup olive oil
Juice of 2 lemons
Salt
Pepper
Tapenade

Pistachio-orange *tapenade*:
1 cup pistachios, shelled
1 teaspoon orange zest
1/3 cup orange juice
1 tablespoon lemon juice
1/2 cup *ammudicata* (see page 24)
2 cloves garlic, chopped
1 teaspoon kosher salt
1/2 cup extra virgin olive oil

To prepare the fish, cut into 3/4-inch to 1-inch thick steaks, and then cut into smaller pieces. Place the fish on a baking sheet, drizzle with some of the oil and lemon juice, and season with salt and pepper. Place about a tablespoon of *tapenade* on each piece of fish. Cook in the oven for 25 to 30 minutes, until the fish is firm and white all the way through. To make the *tapenade*, place the pistachios in a food processor and chop. Add all the other ingredients except the oil to the food processor. Turn on the processor and in a slow, steady stream drizzle in the remaining oil.

Fried Smelt

Smelt is a family of silvery fish found in the cool waters of the Northern Hemisphere. This recipe is not one I usually prepare at home for Saint Joseph's day, but it is a very popular dish with the Sicilian population of Buffalo. Found on a few restaurant Saint Joseph's menus, it is served in place of the more traditional sardines.

2 cups flour
1 tablespoon salt
1 teaspoon black pepper
1/2 teaspoon cayenne
1 tablespoon chili powder
1 teaspoon garlic powder
1 pound smelt fillet
3 eggs
1/2 cup milk
Oil or Crisco (for frying)
Salt
Pepper
Lemon for garnish

Place the flour and seasonings in a gallon plastic storage bag. Add the fish and shake to coat. Pour the coated fish into a strainer to remove the excess flour. Save the flour for a second coating. Mix the eggs and milk and dip the fish in the mixture to coat. Return the fish and the flour to the bag and recoat the fish. Heat enough oil to cover the bottom of a large pan. Add the fish and sauté until golden brown, about 1 minute per side. Remove the fish to paper towels or brown paper to drain the excess oil. Season the smelt generously with salt and pepper and garnish with lemon.

Dolci/Desserts

Mama Dano's Chocolate Cookies

Anise Cookies

Cannoli

Cucidati (Fig Cookies)

Pignocatta (Pinecone Pastry)

Sesame Cookies (Giordano Cookies)

Pizzelle

Sfinge di San Giuseppe

Zeppole di San Giuseppe

Chocolate *Tartufi* (Truffles)

Dolci/Desserts

The desserts seem to me to be the most confusing part of the traditional Saint Joseph's day meal. Which ones to serve? They all sound alike. I think the problem lies in the dialects of the regions. Most are variations of the same dessert. *Sfinge di San Giusseppe* is basic pâte a choux dough that makes a fried creme puff. Some stuff the cream puff with a custard or ricotta mix. *Zeppole di San Giusseppe* is also usually a cream puff or a fritter that can be baked or fried and filled with custard or *ricotta*. Some recipes suggest they be coated with honey. *Pignolatti* or *pignoccata* (both spellings are correct) mean pinecone, perhaps in different dialects. This is simple dough rolled into smaller balls than *zeppole* or *sfinge*, coated in honey and orange flavor. I recommend serving a fruit dessert, a cookie, a creme puff, and the honeyed pinecone.

Mama Dano's Chocolate Cookies

Preheat oven to 375°F.

3 3-ounce packages cream cheese
1 cup Crisco
1-1/2 cups sugar
1 cup milk
3 large eggs, beaten
1-1/2 teaspoons vanilla
1 cup cocoa powder

5 cups flour
1 teaspoon cinnamon
1/2 teaspoon ground cloves
5 teaspoons baking powder
2 cups raisins
1 12-ounce bag semi-sweet chocolate chips
1 cup chopped nuts (optional)

Blend the cream cheese, shortening, and sugar together using an electric mixer. Add the milk, eggs, and vanilla to the mixture and blend together. In a separate bowl, combine all the dry ingredients. Slowly add the dry ingredients to the cream cheese blend until incorporated. Add the raisins, chips, and nuts. Roll the mixture into balls slightly smaller than golf balls. Place on an ungreased cookie sheet at least 1 inch apart. Bake at 375°F for 10 to 15 minutes. Cookies should be slightly soft when removed from the oven. Dust with confectioners' sugar, or use the frosting in the cucidati recipe on page 110.

Anise Cookies

Preheat oven to 375°F.

This recipe is from Louise Bozzini Giordano, my father's first cousin on his fathers' side. Her son is my cousin Gary, who lives in San Francisco. I have yet to meet him, but I think we'd get along well!

5 large eggs
2 cups sugar
2 teaspoons vanilla
1 cup Crisco (or butter or butter Crisco)

2 teaspoons anise extract
3 tablespoons milk
4 cups flour (more if needed)
6 tablespoons baking powder

Beat the eggs. Add the sugar and vanilla, beat until creamy. Add the Crisco. Beat until light and airy. Add the anise extract and milk. Blend in the flour and baking powder. Form into little ovals. Bake for 10 minutes at 375°F.

Cannoli

Shells:
3 cups flour
1/4 cup sugar
1 teaspoon cinnamon
2 tablespoons butter, cubed
1 extra-large egg
1/4 cup sweet Marsala
1 tablespoon white vinegar
1 tablespoon water
Cannoli tubes
Cooking oil for frying
2 egg whites (for sealing)

Filling:
2 pounds ricotta (Sorrento whole
  milk supreme, not part skim)
1 cup whipped cream
2 cups confectioners' sugar
2 tablespoons orange zest
2 tablespoons lemon zest
2 tablespoons vanilla
1 cup mini semi-sweet chocolate chips
Pistachios, ground (optional)

To make the shells, sift together the dry ingredients. Cut the butter into the dry ingredients. Make a well and pour in the wet ingredients. Using a fork, slowly blend the wet ingredients into the dry ingredients a little at a time. When blended, knead the dough for a couple of minutes, wrap in plastic wrap, and allow it to rest in the refrigerator. Divide the dough into 3 or 4 pieces and roll out using a pasta maker (No. 5 or 6) or a rolling pin. Cut out circles about 5 inches in diameter, using a circle cutter or a water glass.

Roll the circles of dough around the metal tubes and seal the edges with egg white. Heat about an inch of cooking oil in a pan large enough to hold 3 to 4 shells at a time. Regulate the heat so it continues to bubble while the dough cooks, but does not smoke. When the shells are done, remove them to a plate covered with paper towels to drain. When the shells are cool enough to touch, remove the tubes and repeat.

Shells may be made as many as 4 or 5 days ahead and stored in a sealed container.

To make the filling, combine all the ingredients except the pistachios and blend well. Using a pastry bag, fill each shell from both ends, making sure the filling meets in the middle. If you like, dip the ends of the cannoli in ground pistachios. Candied fruit can also be added to the ricotta mix.

Cannoli and Stuffed Sfinge

Cucidati (Mama Dano's Fig Cookies)

Preheat oven to 350°F.

Filling:
1 pound pitted dates, chopped
1 orange with skin, chopped
1/2 cup lemon juice
1/2 pound candied fruit
2 pounds figs, stems removed
1/2 cup honey
1/2 cup water
1 pound raisins
1 pound walnuts, chopped
1 14-ounce bag semi-sweet chocolate chips
1 teaspoon cinnamon
1 teaspoon ground cloves
1 shot brandy

Dough:
7 cups flour
Pinch salt
6 rounded tablespoons baking powder
1-1/2 cups butter
1-1/2 cups sugar
4 large eggs
1 tablespoon vanilla
1 cup cold water

Frosting:
1-1/2 cups confectioners' sugar
2 tablespoons milk
2 teaspoons almond extract
4 tablespoons butter, softened

To make the filling, blend the first seven ingredients in batches in a food processor. Remove from the processor and cook the mixture in a heavy-bottomed pot for about 5 minutes on low heat to melt. Blend the melted mixture together. Cool the mixture and mix in the remaining six ingredients.

To make the dough, sift together the flour, salt, and baking powder. In a separate bowl, cream the butter, sugar, eggs, and vanilla, using a mixer. Add the water and mix. Gradually add the flour blend. Roll out the dough into 4-inch wide, 1/8- to 1/4-inch-thick rectangles. Place filling down the middle of the rectangles, fold, seal, and cut on the bias in 2-inch lengths. Bake for 10 to 15 minutes at 350°F. Cookies should be a bit soft when removed from the oven.

To make the frosting, mix all the ingredients with a spoon. When the *cucidati* are cool, frost and decorate with multi-colored or chocolate sprinkles.

Cucidati preparation

Pignocatta (Pinecone Pastry)

These delicious pinecone pastries are also known as *pignolatti*.

3 cups flour
4 eggs at room temperature
Pinch of salt
1 orange, peeled and juiced

1/2 cup sugar
1/2 cup honey
Oil for frying

Mix together the flour, eggs, and salt, and knead for 2 to 3 minutes. Wrap the dough in plastic wrap and set aside. Squeeze the juice from the orange and reserve. Cut the orange peel into julienne strips and reserve to use for garnish. Combine the sugar, honey, and juice in a medium saucepan. Cook over medium heat until melted and well blended. Heat about 2 inches of oil in a frying pan. Cut off small portions of dough and then roll it into pencil-like logs. Cut into 1/4-inch pieces to produce pea-sized balls and fry in the oil until golden brown. Remove the balls with a slotted spoon. Drain on absorbent paper and allow to cool. Drop the balls into the honey glaze, coat, and remove with the slotted spoon. Pile the balls on a serving platter to build a pinecone. Garnish with the reserved orange peel.

Sesame Cookies (Giordano Cookies)

Our name, Giordano, originated with the First Crusade in 1095 A.D. with Sicilian foot soldiers under the Sicilian-Norman knights, Tancredo and his vassals. One goal of the foot soldiers was to "see the Jordan River" and be baptized again. When these peasant soldiers returned to their homeland, their family names became Jordan, Gordon, and, in Sicily and Italy, Giordano. Today in Jordan, the most popular cookie sold is made with sesame seeds just as it was during biblical times. We include this recipe to pay homage to our ancestors who gave us our family name.

Preheat oven to 375°F.
Makes 6 to 8 dozen cookies.

5 extra-large eggs
2 cups sugar
1 cup Crisco
1 teaspoon vanilla extract
1 teaspoon anise extract
3 to 6 tablespoons milk
4 to 5 cups flour
4 tablespoons baking powder
1/2 cup honey, warm
1/2 cup sesame seeds

Use a mixer to beat the eggs and sugar until creamy. Add the Crisco and beat until light and fluffy. Add the vanilla, anise, and 3 tablespoons of the milk. Gradually add the flour and baking powder and blend. If the batter is too dry, add more milk one tablespoon at a time. Remove the batter from mixer and roll into 4 to 5 6-inch-long logs that are about 1-1/4-inch in diameter. Wrap each log in plastic wrap and refrigerate for several hours or overnight.

Unwrap the dough, cut it into 1/4-inch slices, and place the slices on parchment-lined cookie trays. Spread softened honey on the cookies, using a teaspoon, and cover with sesame seeds. Bake for 22 to 26 minutes at 375°F. Longer cook time produces crispier cookies.

Pizzelle

It is generally believed that *pizzelle* originated in the middle region of Italy during ancient times to mark an annual celebration. Initially baked over an open fire with relatively simple but effective irons, early *pizzelle* often were proudly embossed with the family crest or some indication of the village of origin. Over time it became a tradition to use *pizzelle* to celebrate any holiday or festive occasion, but inevitably there were *pizzelle* for everyone at Christmas and Easter. The modern patterns found on these delicious waffle cookies most commonly are floral on one side and a woven basketlike pattern on the other. The recent increased popularity of *pizzelle* is the result of greater recognition of their delicious versatility. For example, *pizzelle*, when still hot, can be formed into cylinders, cones, and minibaskets that can hold a wide variety of delicious fillings for festive occasions. The range of taste experiences that can be created with fillings of formed *pizzelle* is virtually endless.

Makes 150 *pizzelle*.

6 eggs
1/2 cup vegetable oil
2 teaspoons vanilla or anise extract (pure)
3 cups all-purpose flour
2 teaspoons baking powder
1-1/2 cups sugar

To prepare the batter, beat the eggs until smooth. Add the oil and vanilla. Sift the flour and baking powder together onto the egg mixture. Add the sugar and blend vigorously until smooth, sticky, and stiff. Test by dropping the mixture from a small teaspoon or demitasse spoon. Add a few tablespoons of water until the mix drops as a ribbon in 2 to 3 seconds. If the mix is too thin, add a few tablespoons of flour.

To make the *pizzelle*, set the color control dial of your pizzelle maker to about 3 to 3-1/2 and bake, using the red/green light cycle for timing. Alternatively, bake for approximately 45 seconds, open the lid briefly to examine the color, and bake longer, as desired, to create a darker surface. The baking time can be shortened slightly by increasing the color control dial reading about half a unit.

Sfinge di San Guiseppe

Makes 50 to 60 pieces.

2 cups water
5 tablespoons butter
2 tablespoons sugar
Pinch of salt
2 teaspoons baking powder
2 cups flour
8 large eggs
2 teaspoons vanilla extract
2 teaspoons whiskey
Crisco or vegetable oil for frying
  (Crisco produces a crispier crème puff)
Confectioners' sugar for garnish
Orange peel for garnish

Sfinge have a life of their own. Once you release them into the hot oil, they flip themselves over again and again until they are almost done. There is no need to touch them at all except at the very end when they won't turn over anymore. Then, help them out with one last flip before removing them to a paper towel to drain.

Bring the water, butter, sugar, and salt to a boil in a large saucepan. Add the baking powder and flour all at once and stir until the mixture comes away from the sides of the pan. Remove the pan from the heat and allow it to cool for 2 minutes or until the mixture is no longer steaming. Place the mixture in a food processor, and turn the machine on. Add the eggs one at a time, processing them until they are incorporated. Add the vanilla and whiskey, blending them into the mixture.

Heat 2 to 3 inches of oil to 375°F in a deep fryer or a large, shallow pot. The dough will expand to 2 or 3 times its original size, so be sure to use sufficient oil. Drop batter into the oil 1 teaspoon at a time, and fry until golden brown. Remove the puffs to drain on paper towels. Fill the puffs with custard or ricotta (see page 108), and sprinkle them with confectioners' sugar when ready to serve. Garnish with candied orange peel.

Zeppole di San Giuseppe

Preheat oven to 450°F.

These cream puffs aren't fried like the custard-filled zeppole you find at bakeries, but I think they taste better.

Puffs
1 cup hot water
1/2 cup butter
1 tablespoon sugar
1/2 teaspoon salt
1 cup sifted all-purpose flour
1 tablespoon baking powder
4 eggs
1 teaspoon grated orange peel
1 teaspoon grated lemon peel

Ricotta filling
(See page 108. Make half-batch)

To make the puffs, lightly grease a baking sheet. Bring the water, butter, sugar, and salt to a boil in a medium saucepan. Add the flour and baking powder all at once, and beat vigorously with a wooden spoon until the mixture leaves the sides of the pan and forms a smooth ball, about 3 minutes. Remove the pan from the heat. Quickly add the eggs, 1 at a time, beating until the mixture is smooth after each addition. Continue beating until the mixture is smooth and glossy. Add both peels and mix thoroughly. Drop the batter by tablespoons 2 inches apart on the baking sheet. Bake at 450°F for 15 minutes. Lower the heat to 350°F and bake for an additional 15 to 20 minutes or until golden. Remove puffs to a rack and cool completely. Cut a slit in the side of each puff and fill with whipped cream, vanilla pudding, or ricotta filling.

Chocolate *Tartufi* (Truffles)

Quick, easy, and delicious.

16 ounces of a good quality chocolate semi-sweet, dark, milk chocolate or any combination.
1-1/2 cups heavy cream
4 tablespoons butter
2 tablespoons liqueur of choice (Grand Marnier, Frangelico)

For the coating:
Cocoa powder
Ground nuts of your choice (almonds, walnuts, pistachios)
Grated, toasted coconut
Confectioners' sugar

Chop chocolate chips or bars into half-inch pieces and place in a bowl. Heat cream and butter to the boiling point. Pour the mixture over the chocolate and let stand for 5 minutes. Whisk the chocolate mixture until smooth and add the liqueur. Refrigerate the mixture until it is firm. Form 1-inch balls and roll them in any of the coatings: cocoa, ground nuts, coconut, or confectioners' sugar. Refrigerate until needed. Serve at room temperature.

Party-planning Check Lists

The Decorations and Table Essentials
The Food
The Invitation
The Small Gift
The Speakers and Prayers
The Prep List
The Shopping List
Source List

It is customary to give guests a small gift of bread to take home with them. We fill small brown paper bags with a couple of fava beans, a Saint Joseph's prayer card, a small roll, and an orange.

The Decorations and Table Essentials

Altar with 3 steps

Saint Joseph Statue or Picture

Lace Tablecloth and Doilies

Plates and Silverware

Ceramic Bowls and Platters for Buffet

Serving Utensils

Votive Candles

Dried Fava Beans

Vases of Wheat/Dried Spaghetti

Floral Arrangements (Lilies)

Fresh Fruit for Display

Gift for Guests

Saint Joseph's Day Prayer

Speaker to explain the tradition, the menu,
  and the prayer

Other traditions to be included

Beverages and Glasses

Menu

Shopping list

Invitations

Prep list

The Giordano Saint Joseph's Table Menu

Lentil Soup
Pasta con Sarde
Baked Cod with Lemon and Tomatoes
Marinated *Calamari* Salad

Assorted *Froggia:*
  Mushroom/Asparagus/Cauliflower/ Rapini

Saint Joseph's Bread

Olives
Carduni Fritti
Fennel Sliced with Olive Oil and Lemon
Fava Beans and Garlic

Dandelion Greens with Garlic
Stuffed Artichokes Mama Dano
Marinated Eggplant
Roasted Red Pepper Salad
Marinated Mushrooms
Pickled Beets

Fresh Fruit Displays:
  Whole and Sliced Oranges, Bananas, Grapes,
  Apples. Kumquats

Sfinge
Cannoli
Pignolatti

Acknowledgments

I must first thank Saint Joseph. In fact this entire book is a thank you to him for granting my wish when I prayed to him to bless my family with a child. That child would be my daughter, Gabriella, who I thank for being my special bit of luck, my granted favor for which I am so grateful.

Great thanks to my father, Dr. Paul B. Giordano, who has always lined up projects for me. He was very persistent about this one, however. He led me through the writing of the book, getting me back on track when I veered off. Thanks also to my father's wife, Marian, who helped us every step of the way, testing recipes, reading, cooking and taking care of all the details for the parties: the lace, the flowers, the goodie bags, desserts, decorations – even the clean-up!

Thanks to my partner, Heather Harmon, for her unending patience with me and my preoccupation with this project for so long.

Thanks to Nica Jadoch and Jonelle Marchese for photographing the many parties and for commiserating with me on style and content.

Thanks to David and Wendy Schutte and to Silvia and Bob Fredericks , for supporting, reading, and contributing family recipes and other stories and prayers. Special thanks also to David Schutte for allowing me to test so many recipes at the Creekview restaurant.

Thanks to my cousin Mary Ellen Juliano for making cookies with us and improving our *cucidati* recipe.

Thanks to my mother for reading the book cover to cover, every time I asked her to.

Thanks to Carl Falletta for his guidance and experience.

Thanks to Kevin Telaak for hosting the book launch, and to Christa Glennie Seychow for her support.

Thanks to Ramona Whitaker for her detailed editing, and to Dr. Mark Donnelly for designing a book that is just as I envisioned it, only better. Special thanks to my publisher, Marti Gorman, for making it all a reality.

To all of my fathers' and my friends and family who attended all of the *tavolas di San Giuseppe* over the years -- we love you all. Thanks for encouraging us!

Thanks also to my idols: my grandmothers, Josephine Giordano and Lucille Falbo and also Daniel Brownstein. You taught me that I can do anything I put my mind to.

The process of completing the Saint Joseph's Day Table Cookbook was like a map that I had to follow. These are just some of the many people who led me on this marvelous journey.

References

Cucina di Sicilia, by Paola Andolina, Dario Flaccovio Editoria, 1990.

Cucina Siciliana: Authentic Recipes and Culinary Secrets from Sicily, by Clarissa Hyman, (Northampton, MA: Interlink Books, 2007).

Father Pat's Place: A Catholic Priest of the Diocese of La Crosse, www.frpay.com.

The Food of Lovers Companion, 2nd Edition, Sharon Tyler Herbst, (Barron's Educational Services, Inc., 1995).

The Food of Southern Italy, by Carlo Middione, (New York: William Morrow and Company Inc, 1987).

The Heart of Sicily: Recipes & Reminiscences of Regaleali, a Country Estate, by Anna Tasca Lanza (Clarkson Potter, 1993).

Living the Catholic Life, www.Catholic culture.com.

Mimmetta Lo Monte's Classic Italian Cooking, by Mimmetta Lo Monte (New York: Simon and Schuster, 1990).

Saint Joseph's Table, Initaly.com/regions/sicily/joetabl.htm.

Sicilian Home Cooking: Family Recipes from Gangivecchio, by Wanda and Giovanne Tornabene with Michele Evans (New York: Knopf, 2001).

Sicily: Culinary Crossroads, by Giuseppe Coria (New York: Oronzo Editions, 2008).

Swallows of Capistrano, www.sanjuancapistrano.net/swallows/

Viva San Giuseppe: A Guide for Saint Joseph Altars, (New Orleans: Saint joseph Guild, 1985).

"Tasty recipes for special March days", by Janice Okun, the Buffalo News, Monday, March 5, 1984, page D-2.

A Year in a Vegetarian Kitchen: Easy Seasonal Dishes for Family and Friends, by Jack Bishop, (New York: Houghton Mifflin, 2004).

Index

Index